Hi Louise,

I thought

have a copy of my new book...

so here it is!

The Sandwich That Changed My Life!

Enjoy,

Steve Jenne

Steve Jenne

Steve Jenne
The Sandwich That Changed My Life!

ISBN 978-0-9986367-5-7

Cover Design/Layout: Paula Underwood Winters

Printed in the United States of America

Published by: England Media
102 Rachels Ct
Hendersonville, TN 37075

CONTENTS

Have you ever had a really great sandwich?

I mean a sandwich that was so delicious and mouth-watering that you exclaimed, “Wow! This sandwich is life changing!”

Yeah. Me neither.

But there was this one sandwich.

I didn’t eat it. I never even tasted it.

But I guess you could say it did change my life. It sure did make my life a lot more interesting.

– Steve

DEDICATION

When biographer Scot England called and asked if I could write the "Dedication" to this book, I told him, "Sure, that'll be easy." I could only think of dedicating it to my parents, Loren and Hazel Jenne. They are mentioned prominently throughout the following pages.

To me, being brought up by Mom and Dad seemed almost like a Norman Rockwell setting, depicting my childhood rearing in a small town, Sullivan, in central Illinois, in a house that Dad built himself.

After graduating from high school there, my folks supported me throughout my college years at Central Missouri, then came the Army, including a "tour" in Vietnam, followed by a 31-year career with a consulting engineering firm, and a stint as a co-owner in a restaurant business.

Sandwiched between those years was an almost unbelievable chain of events, which became the impetus for this book. Did I just say "sandwiched"? Consider that to be a little clue as to what you are about to read. Just remember, though, that without my Mom and Dad, none of those events would have been possible.

SEPT. 22, 1960 – SULLIVAN, ILLINOIS

What a thrill it is for a 14-year-old boy! My Boy Scout troop and I are in charge of guarding the Vice President of the United States!

It seems like every person in Sullivan is here in the park. And now they're trying to squeeze through our "security line" to get to Richard Nixon.

Here he comes. He's sitting down at the picnic table right in front of me. I can't believe I'm standing right behind him.

I wish I could get an autograph or photo with him. It would be nice to have a special memento of this grand occasion. But I'm stuck here, holding back the crowd.

It looks like the Vice President is enjoying his buffalo barbecue sandwich. But his wife Pat doesn't seem to be a fan. I don't think she likes it. After a quick bite or two, they're getting up.

"Hey, look. He left his sandwich," I silently say to myself.

My mind starts to race. "No one else sees it. They're all chasing Nixon, trying to get an autograph. Maybe I should pick it up....No, you might get caught....oh go ahead! Just grab it!"

In the next moment, I made a move that would ultimately lead me all the way to Johnny Carson's Tonight Show. And now…60 years after my decision to "grab and go", you are reading my story.

– Steve Jenne

CHAPTER ONE – CHILD OF THE 50S

I thought I had the greatest parents in the world. My father, Loren Jenne was an extraordinary man. He graduated from Eastern Illinois University with a B.S. and M.S. in Education. He started his career as a teacher in the small town of Alvin, Illinois, north of Danville, but just a year later, he got drafted by the Army.

World War II was ongoing, and Dad would serve his country in the Army Air Forces, first as an airplane mechanic. Then, he worked his way into pilot training. A short time later, he was a First Lieutenant flying B-25 Mitchell bombers. He completed 50 bombing missions, from North Africa to Italy.

In 1943, Dad came back home to Illinois, where he married my mom “Hazel” on December 29th at the Sullivan United Methodist Church. Dad resumed his teaching career at the little country school Jonathon Creek, just east of Sullivan. Then, he moved to the Sullivan schools, where he became principal of the Powers, Lowe and Jr. High Schools. In his free time (said sarcastically), Dad also served as Moultrie County Treasurer.

While he continued his education career, Dad also found time to serve 32 years in the military. He retired as a full Colonel and was on active duty during World War II, Korea and during the Vietnam era. He earned numerous military honors including three Bronze Stars and seven Air Medals.

Mother was a homemaker, and had a unique sense of humor. She once sewed up the fly on Dad's boxer shorts! Mom worked a short time as a secretary in the County Clerk's office at the Sullivan Courthouse. Her working 'resume' might not have been as impressive as Dad's was, but she was an impressive woman in her own right. Of course, she was always there to help and support Dad in everything he did. As I write this book, my mother is alive, and will turn 100 years old in November 2020.

Mother's life changed forever on August 31, 1946…the day I was born.

We lived with my Grandma Jenne, Dad's mom, until Dad built a house at 1123 E. Jackson Street in Sullivan. Sullivan sits in Central Illinois and is about 45 miles southwest of Champaign. It's situated between Champaign and Springfield, the hometown of President Abraham Lincoln. In the '40s, '50s and '60s, 75% of Sullivan's economy came from farming corn and soybeans.

One of my first memories is from when I was four years old. One of the great traditions in the town of Sullivan is an event called "Turkey Bingo". For many decades, each year just before Thanksgiving, the Sullivan Lion's Club has hosted the "Turkey Bingo" fundraiser. It still goes on today. These days, they give away frozen turkeys to anyone who wins a bingo game. But back in the day, they gave away LIVE turkeys! Can you imagine trying to load a live turkey into your car for the trip home? Talk about a major prize!

There are a few stories that some of the older people of Sullivan swear are true, that there was a time when they actually threw live turkeys off the top of the Moultrie County Courthouse! I'm sure PETA would have had a big Thanksgiving in Sullivan back then.

While I wasn't around for flying turkeys, I can attest that our Lion's Club did indeed award live turkeys at the early bingo games. I know because my family won one! Dad was a member of the Lion's Club. In 1950, he was the bingo number caller and Mom won a game, and yes, a live turkey. We managed to get the big bird home safely, but while most of the bingo prizes ended up on Thanksgiving dinner plates, ours did not. My sister Lynette and I wouldn't let Mom cook it. We made a pet out of the turkey, and gave it the very original name of Tom. You can actually see a picture of Tom in the photo section of this book.

While Dad went along with his kids' request of having a pet turkey, he could also be pretty strict. Some of my friends later told me that they were afraid of him, and I always tried to be on my best behavior when I was around him. And it seemed that I was always around him! At church, he was my Sunday school teacher and when I went to my regular school, he was my principal. Years later when I went into the military, Dad was a bird Colonel and he actually swore me into the Army at the induction center in St. Louis in 1969.

I started Kindergarten in Sullivan in 1952. Miss Montoni was my teacher, and she was one of my favorites. A year later, due to my Dad's military commitments, we had to move to Solvang, California. My dad was a Captain and Commanding Officer of the National Guard in Sullivan. I started the first grade in Solvang, but I finished the year back in Sullivan when Dad was transferred back to Illinois.

Way back in the 1940s, my Grandpa Jenne predicted that one day people would be able to see moving televised pictures in our homes. His prediction came true in the early '50s when my family got one of the first television sets in Sullivan. Dad was big into electronics, and he was able to rig up his own channel changer that would rotate the outside antenna to get better reception.

I bought my own lawn mower and spent my summers mowing lawns. I also had a paper route. To deliver the *Champaign News-Gazette*, I bought my own bicycle. During the winter months, I made money shoveling snow, but I don't think I bought my own shovel.

Since Dad was the Jr. High Principal, on a day when we got a big, heavy snow, he had to call the radio station WLBH in Mattoon to tell them that school was being cancelled. All the kids (and their parents) listened to the station to see if they had to go to school. The kids all silently prayed they would hear, "No school today in Sullivan." But I always knew it was going to be cancelled a few minutes before it ever got announced on the radio. I would run down Pifer's Lane and start going door to door, offering to scoop sidewalks and driveways. I would be hard at work while my school pals were still sitting by the radio, waiting to hear if school was going to be open.

The 1950s really were a fun time, and Sullivan was a great place for a young boy to grow up. The town of 3,943 was very safe, with almost no crime. Most people left their cars unlocked, many with the keys still inside, and a lot of people also didn't bother locking their doors at home.

The one downside to the small town was that it could sometimes get a little boring, with not a whole lot to do. However, in September of 1960, things would get very exciting. A very well-known man was coming to town, and he was going to have a meal there....a meal that would change my life.

CHAPTER TWO – NIXON

In 1858, Abraham Lincoln came to Sullivan, supposedly to debate Stephen A. Douglas. The two were running for the U.S. Senate. Both candidates had agreed to the event, but instead of a debate, the town got a riot. When the candidates arrived in town, their supporters were in such an uproar, with so much hatred toward the other side, that the debate was called off. The two candidates did speak in Sullivan but at separate locations and at different times. A brass band of Lincoln supporters appeared while Douglas was giving his speech, and they played so loudly that Douglas refused to finish his address.

So, I guess after the "success" of that political debate, the town of Sullivan wanted to try it again 102 years later! The Sullivan Chamber of Commerce hoped the community could host a debate between Vice President Richard Nixon and Senator John F. Kennedy. The two were locked into a very close battle to see who would become the next President of the United States in 1960.

A small group of town leaders traveled to both the Democratic and Republican National Conventions, hoping to get an in-person meeting with Senator Kennedy and Vice President Nixon. A few young Republicans from Sullivan also attended the National Convention in July of 1960. That event was held at the International Amphitheatre in Chicago.

Sullivan residents Leland Glazebrook, Bob Livergood, Paul Romano, Jim Rhodes, and Bill Stubblefield were among those who traveled to the Windy City. The group didn't have any tickets, passes or credentials to get in, and for a while they just stood outside. Then they saw State Senator Red Graham, who was from Charleston, walking in. When they explained their situation to him, Senator Graham yelled, "Let the delegation from Illinois through!"

That got the Sullivan group inside, but they spent most of the night continually walking, so they would not get stopped by someone who wanted to see their credentials. Their constant moving helped get them an up-close view of Richard Nixon, but they were not able to actually speak to him.

The Sullivan "delegation" didn't get a meeting with Nixon in July, but a month later, on August 26th, Congressman William Springer made the official invitation to the Vice President.

A week later, on September 2nd, Nixon officially confirmed that he would be coming to Sullivan! The Sullivan leaders couldn't believe it. But their excitement was dampened four days later, when John Kennedy declined the invitation. Organizers got the turn-down via a telegram sent by U.S. Senator Paul Douglas, who said Senator Kennedy couldn't be there, due to previous obligations.

It was decided that Nixon's visit would be the center of a grand buffalo barbecue. Some folks from the Chamber of Commerce had begun raising a few bison on a farm southeast of town. A year earlier, Sullivan had hosted a buffalo barbecue in Wyman Park, and the turnout was so great that they hoped to make it an annual event.

In August of 1960, the second barbecue brought out 15, 000 people. But as soon as it was over, the town got word that Vice President Richard Nixon wanted to come to Sullivan, so they quickly threw together another "bonus" barbecue for the following month.

Even though Nixon was the only presidential candidate coming to Sullivan, the event was billed as "Political Day". The city leaders wanted it to be non-partisan as they welcomed people from both parties. They didn't care if you were a Kennedy fan or a Nixon supporter. They just wanted you to come spend some time, and hopefully some money in town.

John Ehrlichman was one of the Vice President's advance men. He came into Sullivan the day before the event to make sure all the final arrangements were in place. After

Nixon was elected President, John Ehrlichman became Chief Domestic Advisor to the President and he was in Nixon's inner circle. Ehrlichman later served a year and a half in prison for his role in the Watergate scandal.

Most businesses in town also closed. Some closed at noon, while the Brown Shoe Company and Community Industries, the town's two biggest employers, both shut down for the entire day. They let the schools out for the event, but both the Sullivan and Windsor High School bands performed.

The Vice President flew from Peoria to Decatur. Sullivan's Acting Mayor Bob Livergood and James Ralston, the Chamber of Commerce President, both met Nixon when he landed at the Decatur airport. Ivan Wood, the Mayor of Sullivan, missed the event because he was driving his son Stephen to college in Idaho at the time.

An impressive motorcade then brought Nixon to Sullivan. Bill Stubblefield had a car dealership in town, and just days before the big event, he called the main office of General Motors in Detroit. Bill told them he "needed 12 Buick convertibles for an event in Sullivan, Illinois for the Vice President of the United States." They told him that would be no problem. Then they asked, "Where is Sullivan, Illinois?"

The 12 convertibles were used to bring Nixon and his entourage from Decatur to Sullivan. As the motorcade passed through Dalton City and Bethany, hundreds of residents waited along the highway, hoping to get a glimpse of the Vice President.

Nixon's speech was scheduled to start at 3:00 p.m., and he arrived at the Wyman Park at 2:45. If the Vice President was hoping to be welcomed by a huge crowd, all of his hopes were realized. Most estimates put the crowd size at 17, 000 people. That was a pretty packed park, especially when you consider that the entire town had a population of less than 4, 000 at the time.

With a crowd of that size, you just knew that they had to have the very best security they could afford to help protect the Vice President of the United States. Yes, they spared no expense as they called in…the Boy Scouts! That's where I come in. I was a 14-year-old freshman in high school, and I would be one of the "bodyguards" for the second most powerful man in the world.

Bill Shasteen and Bill Stubblefield were leaders of the Troop 39 Sullivan Boy Scouts. It was a group of about 10 Scouts, and I was one of them. I enjoyed being in the group, but I really didn't excel as a Scout. (I never went on to become an Eagle Scout.) However, our little troop was somehow chosen to help protect Vice President and Mrs. Nixon as they ate their buffalo barbecues in Sullivan!

I wasn't a huge Nixon fan, and I really had nothing against Senator John Kennedy. My Dad, though, was a

Republican, and ran unsuccessfully on the Republican ticket for Superintendent of Schools in 1960. That turned out to be the year for the Democrats, with Kennedy leading the way. Nonetheless, I was honored to help protect our Vice President. Our troop was to be stationed around the picnic table where Nixon and his wife Pat were to be seated.

After seeing the large crowd, the second thing Nixon saw was a huge painting of himself that was the centerpiece of the speaker's platform. Adelyn Romano, Paul Romano's wife, painted the portrait. It dwarfed a big buffalo head that hung just beneath it.

The Business and Professional Women's Club of Sullivan made Pat Nixon an honorary member of the club. The local Chamber of Commerce gave her a big corsage. The Chamber's executive secretary said they borrowed 50 tables and 500 chairs from the Illinois State Fairgrounds in Springfield. And it was "Chamber of Commerce weather". It was a beautiful day in Central Illinois, especially for September when it is usually starting to turn cool.

Harry Page was the person who introduced Nixon. Harry had placed his wristwatch on the podium and as Nixon finished his speech, he gathered his papers and also took Harry's watch. When he realized what he had done, he returned the watch to Harry.

The Vice President's speech took place just two hundred yards from the spot where Abraham Lincoln spoke in 1858.

Nixon concentrated on agriculture during his address. One big factor in Nixon saying "yes" to the invite to Sullivan was because it was the hometown of Charles Shuman. At the time, Shuman was the President of The American Farm Bureau Federation. He was also the most well-known person from Moultrie County.

Nixon spent most of his address lauding local farmers and talking about how the agricultural community affects the whole world. After his speech, Nixon and his wife headed to the picnic table where I was standing guard, along with my nine Boy Scout pals. Our job was to keep the large crowd back. That was quite a job as everyone was pushing forward, trying to get a look at the Nixons, especially after they sat down at the table.

Luckily, a few "real bodyguards" from the Secret Service were also standing by, keeping an eye on everything. But you have to remember that this was before the Kennedy assassination, and security around the political leaders was not at all like it would become a short time later.

The Vice President and his wife Pat sat down right in front of me, with their backs to me. I never said anything to Nixon, and I never shook his hand. I took my "security" job very seriously.

While I was assigned to security duty, 10-year-old Janet Rhodes had a much more glamorous job. She was the person who presented the Vice President with his sandwich.

I was four years older than Janet, and I didn't really know her at all. Over the years, I actually never had a conversation with her. But as I was working on this book, I wondered what she remembered about the barbecue. I didn't even know if she was still alive. Most of the people who played major roles on that day are all gone now, but since Janet was just 10 at the time, I thought there might be a good chance she was still around.

Since Janet's father was one of the main organizers of the event, I knew she would have some great insight about the occasion. After reaching out to the folks at the Moultrie County Historical Society, they were able to find that Janet was indeed alive and well and living in Florida. I'm sure she was a little surprised to get our call! But I thought it would be fun to include some of Janet's memories of that day:

"I cannot believe 60 years have passed! In my mind, I shouldn't be as old as I am!

My father, James, had the Rhodes Lumber Company on Route 121 in Sullivan. For the first 16 years of my life, our family lived in the upstairs of the lumber yard.

Dad was very active in the community. He had been President of the Chamber of Commerce. He was also chair of the Moultrie County Democratic party. He was a serious Democrat! My father and some other local men went to both the Democratic and Republican conventions. They went to them hoping to meet with John F. Kennedy and Richard

Nixon so they could personally invite them to Sullivan for a big debate.

While he was excited when Nixon agreed to come, it really aggravated him that Senator Kennedy declined because of scheduling problems.

It was my Dad's idea to make the event a buffalo barbecue. He raised buffalo. He traveled to South Dakota to buy them. He took care of them and treated many of them as his pets. My family kept the herd on land that was across from the lumber yard. Later, the Hezzy's bowling alley and restaurant were built on that site. Dad later moved the buffalo out to some land where the sewage treatment plant is now.

Dad thought the uniqueness of a buffalo barbecue would draw people into town. He was always trying to come up with ideas to promote the town and the small businesses of Sullivan, and was always looking for ways to help the town merchants.

Paul Romano was co-chair of the event with my Dad. But I'm sure it wasn't Dad's idea for me to present the sandwich to Nixon. But the planning committee thought it would be something I could do. Since I was going to have direct contact with the Vice President, I got to have my own Secret Service agent. My parents went to Decatur to meet Nixon's plane and bring him to Sullivan. But I was left in Sullivan with this big security man. He stayed with me and told me to have fun and smile big when I met Nixon.

But even at the age of 10, I wasn't a fan of Nixon. I'm sure my father's politics had already influenced me and I was a Kennedy fan! When I gave him his sandwich, Nixon never said anything to me. But his wife talked to me for a long time. She was very nice and really gracious, as she talked to me about her children. She told me one of her daughters was close to my age.

It's been a long time since I was in Sullivan. I moved to Florida 40 years ago. When I moved, I brought along a huge collection of memorabilia from that day in 1960. But I'm afraid it has a very sad ending.

My father paid a professional photographer to take photos of Nixon's visit to Sullivan. The photos were all just amazing. He also hired a guy to film the entire event. He filmed the entire speech and everything before and after.

When I moved to a home on the beach, I wanted to keep my collection safe from any possible hurricanes. So I put it all in a big closest. But three years ago, my house burned to the ground. My husband died in the fire. My two dogs also perished in the blaze. And all of the Nixon photos and the video were destroyed. My newspaper articles and my letter from Nixon were all burned up. I had a huge container full of items and it's all gone.

I do have one item from that day. I have the dress I wore that day. My mother had saved it all those years. I didn't even know she had kept it. When she had to go into a nursing home, I found it in one of her drawers. I put it in my mother's old cedar chest and covered it with my aunt's crocheted bedspread. When our house burned, that bedspread acted as a fire retardant and it saved that dress.

With my father being a lifelong Democrat, it was pretty ironic that I was chosen to be the person who gave him his meal. But Dad was proud of that day. He always had framed pictures of the event in our house. My father was never one to brag about anything. He didn't talk about his large role in the whole thing. But his big regret was not being able to get Kennedy there.

I still tell people about that day with Nixon. When I'm at an event and I'm asked to tell about any memorable event in my life, I often choose that day." – Janet Rhodes Hamer

I thank Janet for sharing her memories here. She was 10 years old in 1960. Now she's 70. At the time, I was 14, and today I'm 74. We were two of the youngest people who played any kind of role that day. Unfortunately, all of the people who played much larger parts were, of course, older than we were, and now almost all of them are gone.

Ellsworth Lehman and Jack Harshman were in charge of the barbecue itself, and Ed Kohlrus was the man who actually cooked the meat. He barbecued six whole bison for the feast.

After Janet Rhodes gave the Nixon's their buffalo barbecue sandwiches, both said they had never eaten buffalo before. The Vice President held up his sandwich and then took a big bite. Then he said simply, "Very good!" His wife Pat was wearing white gloves and she just looked at her sandwich. I don't think she attempted more than a nibble. Richard Nixon took a couple more bites, said it was "very tasty" and then put his sandwich back on a small paper plate.

As they finished their very quick meal, the couple got up to head toward their car. Nixon was mobbed by hundreds of people wanting to shake his hand or get an autograph. I did the best I could to keep everyone from totally engulfing him. As I tried to keep everyone orderly, for some reason, I found myself looking back at the picnic table the Nixon's had just left. I saw the Vice President's half-eaten sandwich still sitting there. No one had bothered to pick it up or throw it away.

I continued doing crowd control as I gradually inched closer to the table. One step later, I stood directly over the forgotten meal.

My 14-year-old mind told me, "This is the chance of a lifetime. Get his sandwich!"

I looked around and saw that no one was watching me. Everyone was chasing after Mr. and Mrs. Nixon. I was all alone at the table…just me…and the sandwich.

In one swoop, I grabbed the paper plate and sandwich. Another quick look side to side, and a sigh of relief that no one had seen me!

By the way, Nixon was also given a bottled soft drink to, as we said in Sullivan…wash down his sandwich. Nixon might have taken it with him when he got up to leave. But I didn't take the bottle. If it had been left on the table, I probably would have picked it up.

As soon as I could leave my security post, I ran to find my bicycle. Remember in the Willie Wonka movie, when Charlie finally finds the Golden Ticket and he races home with his treasure? Yep, that's exactly what I did too. I held my treasure close to my stomach until I got to my bike; then I rode one-handed all the way home.

When I got home, I threw open the door and yelled, "Mom! Look what I've got!" She asked, "What is it?"

I proudly held it up to her face and proclaimed, "This is the sandwich that HE bit into!

Mom asked, "You took Nixon's sandwich?! What do you want me to do with it?"

I yelled, "Freeze it!"

My mother put the sandwich in a plastic bag, then she gently placed it in a Musselman's Applesauce glass jar. She tightened the lid and put it in our freezer. Mom made a nice bound folder where she said I could store Nixon's paper plate. She wrote "Sandwich Souvenirs" on the outside of the folder; but before she finished the folder, I said, "I want to write something on the plate." These are the words I inscribed: "This is the plate on which Vice President and future President Nixon ate buffalo barbeque. Date Sept 22, 1960." I spelled barbecue with a Q. My prediction of Nixon becoming President did come true, but not in 1960. I (and Nixon) would have to wait almost a decade before he was finally elected, in 1968.

My sister Lynette, 2 years older than I, was already home when I got back from the barbecue. She now lives in Indian Head Park, Illinois. I knew she would have some unique memories of that day, so I asked her to share a few here:

"Sullivan was such a nice place to grow up. It was so clean. It was also a safe and fun place for kids and teenagers. And my brother Stephen was one of the funniest kids to be around. He was funny and was always doing something silly. He liked to play jokes on people. He got his sense of humor from our mother. She liked to play jokes and tell funny stories. Stephen loved sports. He loved baseball and was very active when he was growing up. We were very close as we grew up. I was very protective of him.

The day of the barbecue, I wasn't real close to Nixon. I was about 50 yards from the stage during the speech. The crowd was so huge. But I could see both Nixon and Stephen.

I got home before everyone else. I was in my bedroom, like most 16-year-old girls. When Stephen came home, he burst in the door and he was screaming and running around the entire house, he was so happy.

When I found out why he was so excited, I thought, "That is typical Stephen." I remember that day like it was yesterday…even though 60 years have passed." – Lynette Jenne Drake

A short time after the barbecue, people throughout Sullivan started receiving letters from Washington, D.C. They were "Thank You" letters that Nixon sent to almost every person who was involved in the event. I don't know who handled the Vice President's mail, but they really did an amazing job. Everyone who was in the school bands, the Boy Scouts, the planning committee, and anyone else who helped with the barbecue in any way, received their own letter. Each letter was individualized and worded in different ways. While the Nixon signature is just an autopen, it sure looks real.

There are quite a few people in Sullivan who still have their Nixon letter. Of course, I still have mine! That turned out to be the first of two letters I received from Nixon. The second was not so joyous. He was drafting me into the Vietnam War!

The day after the barbecue, my Mother went to her job at the County Courthouse. She told some of her friends about the "treasure" her son had brought home. One of her friends, Jane Krows, wrote articles for the local newspaper. Mom gave her details of what I had done and Jane put a mention about me in the Sullivan newspaper.

When folks at the bigger newspaper in Decatur read the story, they decided to send a reporter to do a larger story on me. In that article that was published on November 5th, they referred to me as Stephen. (I usually go by "Steve"). They also predicted I would "have a memento to show his grandchildren, barring any extended power failure." Well, the grandchildren never happened, but the power failure did…a couple times! More on that later.

One of the first people I showed the sandwich to was one of my best pals, Phil "Nibs" Best. We were close friends back then and we are still friends today. Phil's Dad, Dr. Best, was originally supposed to be the emcee of the Nixon event, but for some reason, that didn't happen. I thought maybe Phil would know the reason why, so I asked him to share his memories of that day:

"Dad had a lot to do with the planning and organization of the barbecue. Our home was also chosen as the place that Richard Nixon would go if he needed a break or to rest. Our house was just across the road from the park. A couple days before the event, the Secret Service came and walked through our entire home. Nixon never did actually use our home. But a few days after the event, my family received a letter from the Vice President thanking us for making our home available to him.

Dad had planned to be the master of ceremonies for the barbecue. But as was the case almost every day of his career, his schedule was subject to change with very little notice. Dad was the doctor who delivered at least 80% of the population of Sullivan, so I suppose he was called to the hospital at the last minute.

But I was there. I was a Boy Scout with Steve. While Steve stood directly behind Nixon as he sat at the picnic table, I wasn't able to get that close. A lot of the Scouts served as a color guard when Nixon's caravan came into the park. When Nixon gave his speech, I was off to the side and holding an American flag.

A few days after the event, I was at Steve's house. He said, "Hey, I've got something in the freezer I want to show you." He pulled the sandwich out and I said, "OK. You've got a sandwich." He said, "No, it's NIXON'S sandwich!"

Now, 60 years later, I think it's just great that Steve still has that sandwich. I look at it as kind of an honor that I got to see it way back then, when it was still fresh!" - Phil "Nibs" Best

In 1960, Sullivan's main claim to fame was the Little Theatre on the Square. Guy Little Jr.'s theatre was just three years old, but it was already getting a major reputation for bringing in big stars. The biggest star he hired in 1960 was Margaret Hamilton. Sullivan not only had Nixon, but also the Wicked Witch from the Wizard of Oz!

Six decades have now passed since Nixon's visit to Moultrie County. Nixon was the first, and still only, United States Vice President ever to visit Sullivan. Looking back, if it was not *the* very greatest, it was surely *one of* the greatest days in Sullivan's history.

CHAPTER THREE – A NORMAL LIFE...AS A SANDWICH LURKS IN THE FREEZER

When I turned 16 years old, my Dad gave me a 1948, two door Chevrolet Stylemaster. It was black with dull grey interior. The car was a six cylinder with "three on the tree" column shift, and it had a starter button on the floor. Dad bought the car for $100 from a mechanic in Findlay.

I loved that car and I drove it all through high school. Believe it or not, I still have that car today! There was just no way that I could get rid of it, so I still have the first car I ever owned. Not many people can say that.

For a while, I kept that car at an off-site storage facility in Springfield. Then, Dad and I built a 2 1/2 car garage and I put the car in the garage...sideways. I kept it there for more than 20 years. When I finally got it out, I had it towed to Joe Scribner's shop in Sullivan to have it repaired. Joe called a short time later and said they were able to get it started, but something very weird happened. He said, "We couldn't believe the nuts that flew out of that thing!" I thought he meant nuts and bolts. But he meant real nuts! All the years the car was parked in my garage, each winter, squirrels would get in and store the walnuts they had collected in the exhaust pipes! When Joe started the car, nuts shot out like bullets!

In the early 1960s, I worked for The Little Theatre on the Square in Sullivan. The theater owner, Guy Little, Jr., hired me to sell programs outside the show. Little helped "put Sullivan on the map" as he brought in big name television and movie stars to perform at his Little Theatre. One of those stars was David Nelson, Ricky Nelson's older brother. David and his wife came to Sullivan in the summer of 1964.

One day, we got a call at our house from Guy Little. He knew that Dad was a private pilot, who had access to a plane since Dad had started a flying club in Sullivan. Guy told him that David Nelson had never piloted a plane before, but he wanted to take flying lessons. I went with Dad to pick up David, and we drove to the Kirksville airport. It was just a tiny landing strip in the middle of a bean field. But that's where dad gave David his first flying lesson. While Dad was piloting the plane, David sat in the co-pilot seat and I sat right behind him.

When the lesson was finished, my dad, by tradition, gave David his first log book.

David was a really nice guy. He treated me so great and even gave me his phone number and address in Hollywood, but for some reason, I never called or wrote him. Ironically, and sadly, David's brother lost his life in a plane crash on New Year's Eve of 1985.

In October of 1964, when our family moved from Sullivan to Springfield, Dad started the "Flying 20 Club". He eventually bought his own plane. He and I did a lot of flying together over the years. By the way, when our family moved to Springfield, as she was cleaning out our deep freezer, my Mother asked me, "Do you still want this old sandwich? It's four years old!" I answered, "Yes, it's making the move with us."

In addition to getting to know David Nelson, I also got to rub shoulders with another star who came to the Little Theatre. Mickey Rooney loved to entertain…on stage, TV or in the movies. He was also entertaining on the golf course, where I got to see him up close.

Mickey was also an excellent golfer. During his stay in Sullivan, when he wasn't rehearsing or doing his play at the theater, you could find him at the Sullivan Country Club, where I was still a member. The club had a Saturday golf league called "Horse and Rider". The Horse was the low handicap and the Rider was someone who wasn't very good. And I somehow got paired up with Mickey Rooney!

The club had just gotten a brand new Rolls Royce golf cart. It had an electric refrigerator and an AM/FM radio with an 8 track tape player. When I was young, I had a state-of-the-art machine that I used to make my own 8 track tapes. I could plug it into my record player and transfer an album to the 8 track. I made a lot of them and gave them out as presents.

As soon as I got paired with Mickey, I ran to the car and got an 8 track tape that I had made, and Mickey and I and the rest of our foursome listened to the tape as we golfed. We played the round and had so much fun that we planned to do the same the next day. But when heavy rain kept us off the course, we all congregated in the club lounge. I found out that was even more fun than golfing, as Mickey kept us all in stitches with all of his Hollywood stories.

In his life, Mickey Rooney was married eight times! Ironically, I never married...not even once! During my high school years, I dated quite a few girls, but most of them lived in nearby Arthur. (It seemed that Arthur was full of beautiful girls.) But I didn't have a lot of time to date, because I was usually too busy working.

I stacked bread at the IGA every day before school. I also worked at Community Industries, first as a late night-shift janitor, and later, at the Lucy Ellen Candy factory, stacking pallets of starch molds.

I was a much better worker than I was an athlete. While I tried hard, I just wasn't cut out for most high school sports. I was one of the smallest boys in our class. I was 4'9" and weighed just 110 pounds as a freshman. Since I was so small, I got picked on and bullied a lot.

Since I was also working all the time, I couldn't go out for football during my freshman year. Making it to sports practices was a challenge because I had an after-school paper route. However, during my Senior year, I actually earned a letter in football. I also got elected to go to Boys State. This was a big deal! Dr. Best's son, Phil, (who we called "Nibs") and I were both selected to represent Moultrie County at Boys State in Springfield.

At Sullivan High, the best athletes could earn a black T-shirt. If you broke a school record, were on a conference winning team, or if you did something else outstanding in athletics, Coach Bob Calvin gave you a special black T-shirt. You knew the guys who were in the black T-shirts were truly something special. Everyone else (including me) wore red T-shirts. My good pals, Lynn Lowder and Eddie Courtright were both excellent athletes. They were so good that they each earned two or three black T-shirts.

You could also try to accumulate enough points that would qualify you for a black T-shirt. You did that by doing a huge amount of different exercises. I worked hard all of my Senior year and I turned in all my points to Coach Calvin. On the very last day of school, I was in the locker room when Coach Calvin walked up and announced, "Steve, congratulations! You've earned a black T-shirt," as he tossed it to me. I was so proud of that shirt, but I didn't have the chance to wear it to school to show it off, since I got it on the last day of school!

I graduated from SHS in May of 1964. To celebrate, I cruised around the Sullivan square as I blared the Beach Boys song "Fun, Fun, Fun". I got a lot of odd looks as people heard the Beach Boys coming from the radio of a '48 Chevy!

If you would have asked me back in high school what I wanted to be when I grew up, I would have had a very quick answer. My one dream was to be an archaeologist. After all these years, I still have an affinity for archaeology.

In the 1960s, one of the biggest things to happen to Sullivan came when the U.S. Army Corps of Engineers put in Lake Shelbyville. The huge lake covers over 11, 000 acres just a few miles outside of town. To make room for the lake, the Federal government purchased all the farm land and rural homes that were in the area.

When they started making plans to put in the lake, the Corps contracted with the University of Illinois' Department of Anthropology. At one time, the Lake Shelbyville area had seen numerous Indian settlements. It was a very rich area to do salvage archaeology. Nibs Best, Robin Glover and Mike

Shasteen were the original members of the first crew that was hired to dig.

I wanted to be on that crew so bad, and on my lunch break from the candy factory, I drove out to where they were digging. I was covered in sugar and starch from my candy job and I looked like a ghost! I introduced myself to Bill Gardner, who was heading the dig. I begged him for a job, but he said they didn't have enough money. For the next two weeks, each day, I drove back out to the site and repeatedly begged Bill for a job until he finally took me on. My friend Glenn Wright, from nearby Findley was also hired on later that summer.

That was my first archaeology experience, and I stayed with that crew for three years, during the summers of '64, '65 and '66. During our digs, we found post molds of houses, skeletal remains, pottery, refuse pits and projectile points. We had to document and catalogue everything for the University of Illinois in Champaign. Gardner did allow us to spend our lunch break looking for items that we could keep, but they had to be items that were on the surface of the ground; we couldn't dig up anything to keep.

As they began construction of the Shelbyville dam, we knew we were racing against the clock. Once they released the water, everything was going to be lost forever. We wanted to save what we could before they flooded the area.

Today, those Indian settlements are under 20 feet of water at Lake Shelbyville.

In the summer of 1965, a young man named Donald Johanson joined our crew. He was a few years older than the rest of us, but he was needing a job, so Dr. Gardner hired him. Don was a Master's degree candidate at the University of Illinois and then he transferred and got his degree from the University of Chicago.

Nine years after working with us at Lake Shelbyville, Don became well-known around the world. In 1974, he was the anthropologist who discovered "Lucy", the 3 1/2 million-year-old, almost complete hominid skeleton in Ethiopia. He wrote the book "Lucy" and became an overnight sensation as one of the world's most celebrated paleoanthropologists.

Dr. Donald C. Johanson remains one of the most sought-after lecturers on paleoanthropology and human origins. Don and I stayed in touch and have been very close friends since 1965. Twice I was able to get him to lecture at the University of Central Missouri, my alma mater.

My relationship with Central Missouri State began in a unique way. One of my high school friends, John McCown's dad was a traveling salesman. One day during my Senior year of high school, he brought me a brochure about Central Missouri State College in Warrensburg, Missouri, which was primarily a liberal arts college.

My Dad was always big on education. He had a Master's Degree, and he always said he would pay for me to go to my college of choice. After reading their brochure, I thought that Central Missouri was a good fit for me to spend my next four…or five years.

CHAPTER FOUR – COLLEGE

In September of 1964, I started my freshman year at Central Missouri State College, now the University of Central Missouri in Warrensburg, Missouri. I majored in Mass Media, with an English minor. My goal was to work in radio and TV, writing commercials and doing production work.

I was 400 miles away from home, 18 years old, and maybe just a little bit lonesome. Freshmen were not allowed to have cars, but when I became a sophomore, I took my '48 Chevy back to school with me. Dad also had his own plane by then and would often fly in, pick me up and bring me back home to Illinois.

A month after I started college, my parents moved from Sullivan to Springfield. Dad had been promoted to Major in the Army Reserves and he joined the Adjutant Generals Corps within the Selective Service System.

I was supposed to graduate in May of 1968. But in January of that year, the Tet Offensive happened and the

Vietnam War was flaring. One of my college professors said, "Study hard, or you will end up as one of those casualties we read about over in Vietnam."

I knew I was safe, with my 2S deferment while in college, but I intentionally dropped some courses so that I couldn't graduate. I wanted to take just a little more time getting through college. But my Dad was the head honcho with the state of Illinois' Selective Service System! One day he asked me, "What's going on? You should have graduated by now."

He told me, "After you graduate, if you don't go on to get your Master's Degree, your name will go to the top of the draft list."

In November of 1968, when Richard Nixon was elected President of the United States, I was a senior at Central Missouri. I was spending our Thanksgiving break with some TKE fraternity brothers in Florida. I was quite surprised when my Mom called me to say that Jane Krows, the local newspaper reporter, had come by the house.

Now that Nixon was going to finally become President, Jane wanted to know if I still had his sandwich that I had taken back in 1960. I wasn't able to come home, so my Mom took the sandwich out of the freezer and showed it to the reporter. My nephew happened to be there at the time, and Ms. Krows took a photo of my nephew Darren and my Mother with the sandwich. The photo appeared in the local newspaper the following day, and people were amused that I had kept the sandwich for eight years!

But that one newspaper story was it. No one else showed much interest, so for the next 20 years, the sandwich sat quietly in our deep freeze. No one ever asked about it for those two decades. I hardly ever thought about the sandwich myself, as I was too busy enjoying my time (studying!) in college.

I was part of a fraternity, and I enjoyed our keg parties. After my lonely freshman year, my social life seemed to kick into high gear as soon as I got my car (and there were always sorority girls who wanted to take a ride in my '48 Chevy). I dated a lot of girls, but never got real serious with anyone until my senior year. After I graduated, I continued writing to her and I was excited to think about what our future might hold.

CHAPTER FIVE – VIETNAM

I graduated in March of 1969, at the height of the Vietnam War. I had been accepted to grad school at Central Missouri, but I really felt that I owed it to my country to serve in the military. So I let them draft me.

Everyone knew that my Dad was with ~~of~~ the Selective Service System, and they all figured that I would never have to go fight anywhere. They thought I was privileged and that my Dad could pull some strings. However, Dad would never have done something like that, and I would have never expected or accepted that he would use his position in that way.

While I waited to be called up, I went back to the Illinois State Museum. I was so excited when I was told that they had an archaeology job for me. I was put in charge of a dig near a tiny town named Ursa, just north of Quincy, Illinois. My job was to excavate and extract as much as I could before a new bridge was built. I was given a state-owned van, all the tools I needed, and put in charge of the entire project.

I was authorized to hire three laborers to help me with the dig. I traveled to Quincy University and I found three college kids who had an interest in archaeology. I was enjoying that work when I got the letter I figured would eventually come. It was from Uncle Sam, and my old "friend" President Richard Nixon.

Each day when Dad went to work, he would watch my name creep higher and higher up the draft list. He finally came to me and said, "Well, you are probably going to be the next to be called." I said, "That's fine." To be honest, I kind of wanted to go. I wanted to prove myself. I had been in a military family my entire life and I knew this was my turn to carry on the family tradition.

On September 15, 1969, I went into the military. I was to be at the Springfield train depot at 3:00 am. Dad drove me to the station, but I was disappointed that my Mother didn't go with us to see me off. I figured she was so sad that she stayed home. When we arrived, I was surrounded by a bunch of other draftees. Most of them were 18, while I had gone to college for 4 1/2 years.

We took the train to St. Louis, where we took our physical. Then, they took us into a huge room for our swearing in ceremony. But before we took our oath, a Major announced that I was needed in another room. When I walked in, I saw my parents. Dad was in his full uniform! A photographer from the St. Louis Post Dispatch newspaper was also there. My Dad whispered to me, "I am a Colonel, so I ordered this ceremony. I want to be the person who swears in my son."

I quickly found out that a college degree means absolutely nothing when you get drafted. When they chose my MOS (Military Occupational Specialty), two 19-year-olds, both with no college education, interviewed me. They looked at my resume and asked, "What's archaeology?" I answered, "It's where you go dig up dead Indians." They asked what other experience I had. I answered, "Radio and TV with an English minor." One of them laughed, "We don't have much use for a guy who can dig up dead Indians and speak good English." With that, he stamped on my orders, "Infantry." I was assigned 11 Bravo. We called it 11 Bullet.

After extensive training, and a brief stint in Germany, I finally got my orders for Vietnam. I was assigned to the 101st Airborne Infantry Division, also known as "The Screaming Eagles." One day, while in the field on a recon mission, I got a letter from my girlfriend from college. I was almost too excited to even open it!

But my excitement soon turned to heartbreak, as I read my very own "Dear John" letter. She had turned into a full-blown hippie…one who hated the war…and one who hated anyone who was fighting in the war. She actually wrote "I hope you get killed." I dug a hole, burned the letter and buried it. I was happy to get rid of it…and of her.

On April 11, 1971, I spent one of my most memorable Easter Sundays 12,000 miles away from home. I was in the Military Region I ("I" Corps), northernmost sector of South Vietnam. We had no roof over our heads, and it rained all day. Our only travel option was by foot uphill; and drawing fire from an unseen enemy. We were promised that we would be choppered back to the rear for an Easter feast. Our mouths watered as we thought of the menu of hot ham, mashed potatoes and gravy, our choice from numerous side salads, and iced tea, water, soda, or milk.

But the NVA, VC, and Mother Nature had other plans. We never did get what the Army brass had promised us. Instead, we became what was known as "the forgotten patrol". When it was finally found out that we didn't get our Easter feast, the Army made sure that we did get that meal on what was now the following day… in the very early morning hours of Monday, April 12. Our feast turned out to be…leftovers: cold ham, watery mashed potatoes with no gravy, and some lettuce.

To make our special meal even "better", it was served by an overweight cook who was not pleased that he and others had to scurry around to make sure we were properly fed. He angrily growled, "Where were you guys? You were supposed to be here yesterday!" Our whole squad was outraged at his comments. It's hard to forget those times, but in retrospect, I remain thankful to this day that we were even able to survive.

I will always remember another day in 1971. As I stood in formation, in the military command of "at ease", I thought of my three fallen brothers we were memorializing that day. Our C.O., Captain Dooley, choked back his tears as he read aloud the names, dates of birth, and hometowns of three warriors of Charlie Company, 1/506th, 101st Airborne Division, deployed to the Republic of South Vietnam.

In front of our formation were three sets of evenly spaced pairs of jungle boots, with steel helmets and liners placed atop them. No inverted rifle with bayonets plunged into the soil; just boots and helmets. Captain Dooley read a prayer from the printed handout we were all given and asked for a moment of silence. Then a bugler played "Taps", and then we were dismissed. That's how memorial services were conducted back then, over there. Short and never sweet.

Those guys had lost their lives one month earlier, but services were never conducted until our platoon was together "back in the rear" during our stand-down. Less than 48 hours later, we would all be back in the jungle, conducting sweeps and setting up ambushes as members of the Currahee LRRPs, or Long Range Recon Patrols.

My time in Vietnam was made bearable thanks to a very surprising friendship. I was 12,000 miles away from the U.S., trying to get through another very sad day. I had just jumped off a Huey helicopter and onto the tarmac of Firebase Gladiator, in Military Region I ("I" Corps) in the northern sector of South Vietnam. As always, it was raining, hard!, and I was having difficulty getting traction in the wet, red clay, as we walked on an incline, slipping and sliding until I made it to the top.

Through the rain, I heard my first name being called out, from just to my left. I ignored it at first, because seldom was anyone called by their first name . . . usually your last name or a nickname you had acquired while in Vietnam. But then I heard it again, and this time the voice said, "Steve Jenne, Sullivan, Illinois!" I stopped, turned, and focused on one lone soldier, sitting high and dry beneath a shelter, on an ammo box, smoking a cigarette, drinking a beer, and laughing at how I looked, like a drenched rat!

I made my way over to his shelter and saw that it was Wilbur P. McCoy! Wilbur was also from Sullivan, and we went to grade school and high school together. Then we went our separate ways. We hung out with different crowds, and seldom crossed paths. I had pretty much forgotten about Wilbur...but now, here he was in Vietnam.

And what a sight for sore eyes he was, as he quickly offered me a dry cigarette and a cold beer. The ammo box he was sitting on was a home-made cooler, lined with Styrofoam that Wilbur had, ummm, "confiscated". From that moment on, Wilbur and I became inseparable! We shared news and "care packages" from home, including a huge slice of summer sausage he had just received from home. From that day on, Wilbur helped change my whole outlook on life. We looked after each other while on recon patrols and always made sure that the other guy was doing OK. You couldn't find one of us without the other.

There are many stories and movies that involve drugs in the military, specifically by soldiers in combat in Vietnam. I have no doubt that there was much more drug use done by the hippies who didn’t go to Vietnam in the ‘60s and ‘70s. Some of us took great pride in our MOS (the military job to which you are assigned). Mine just happened to be infantry, which is one that no one wanted. I was in the 101st Airborne Division and we were constantly “in the mix”, meaning constant danger.

If we learned that one of our buddies had been smoking pot or taking some kind of hallucinogenic drug, we had a way of taking care of things by ourselves. The problem was alleviated without the trouble and hassle of military courts and judges, and the problem soldier was transferred out of our unit and placed elsewhere…so to speak. Drugs, in my squad/platoon/outfit, were hardly, if ever, abused, once it was learned what the consequences would be.

A few decades have now passed, but I still think about my “tour” in Vietnam. Certain words and objects trigger not-so-fond memories: "wait-a-minute" vines, leeches, foo gas, flechettes, concertina wire, toe poppers, claymores, trip wires, shadows, sounds, and hot LZs. They all still make me cringe.

Eventually, though, I was due to process out of the Army and head for home. Strange as it may seem, I regretted having to leave my buddies there, especially Wilbur McCoy. I had been in Vietnam for a "tour", which had turned into a nightmare.

I left Vietnam, from Cam Ranh Bay and flew to Seattle-Tacoma, Washington. There they gave us an indoctrination where they pressured us to re-enlist. Of course none of us wanted to! As we got ready to leave, one of the leaders sadly stated, "Guys, it's a different world than when you left. You are probably going to encounter some rude people who don't appreciate the service you just gave."

I had no idea what he was talking about…but I was about to find out.

From Seattle, I flew to Chicago O'Hare Airport, still wearing my uniform. I had an aisle seat; the middle seat was empty, and a 40 to 50 year-old woman had the window seat. As soon as I sat down, I started to make conversation with her by saying, "I just got home from Vietnam. It feels so good to be heading home." She said, "Vietnam?" She immediately got up and went up to a stewardess. I saw her point back at me and then they walked her up to a seat in

Family Photo, 1951

With my sister and our pet turkey named Tom

With my school lunch in Solvang, CA. Oct. 1952

Mowing the yard. April, 1953

Playing with my cousin Wayne.

My family after service at the Sullivan United Methodist Church, early 1950s

Family photo. I was 9 years old.

Easter 1955

With my sister Lynette and Dad April 1956

1954

Dreaming of being a football star!

When football season was over, I grabbed my baseball glove and bat.

Basketball in 7th grade at Sullivan Jr. High

Dad leads the Boy Scout troop in the 4th of July parade, 1957.

Three Scouts in Wyman Park. I'm in the middle.

Setting up a cannon display. Bob Beck is on the left.

Moultrie County News

73RD YEAR—NO. 39 | SULLIVAN, ILLINOIS, THURSDAY, SEPTEMBER 22 1960 | 10c PER COPY 2 SECTIONS—SEC. 1

VICE-PRESIDENT AND MRS. RICHARD M. NIXON

Richard M. Nixon to Speak Here Thursday

Vice-President of the United States and Wife to Arrive in Sullivan at 2:45 p.m.; Will Talk in Wyman Park

Vice-President Richard M. Nixon, Republican candidate for President of the United States, will arrive in Sullivan at about 2:45 p.m. Thursday and will make an address at Wyman park at 3:15 p.m.

Mr. Nixon will speak at Sullivan's Political Day Buffalo Barbecue, sponsored by the Sullivan Chamber of Commerce.

The Vice-President is scheduled to arrive at Decatur Municipal airport at 1:50 p.m., where he will be met by a delegation of local and state leaders. Sullivan officials who will welcome the Nixon party at the airport will be: Acting Mayor Robert Livergood; James Ralston, president of the Sullivan Chamber of Commerce; and James Rhodes and Paul Romano, co-chairmen of the celebration.

Wives of the Sullivan delegation will be at the airport to greet Mrs. Nixon, who is accompanying her husband to Sullivan. An 11 vehicle motorcade will escort the party to Sullivan. The Nixon party will arrive at the airport in three Convair planes and Mr. and Mrs. Nixon will be accompanied by Secretary of the Interior Fred Seaton and Senator Hugh D. Scott, Jr., of Pennsylvania.

Among the state officials and [illegible]

Lillian Gustin Wins First | Grand Officers | Fund Drive Completed

It was front page news when the Vice President came to our hometown.

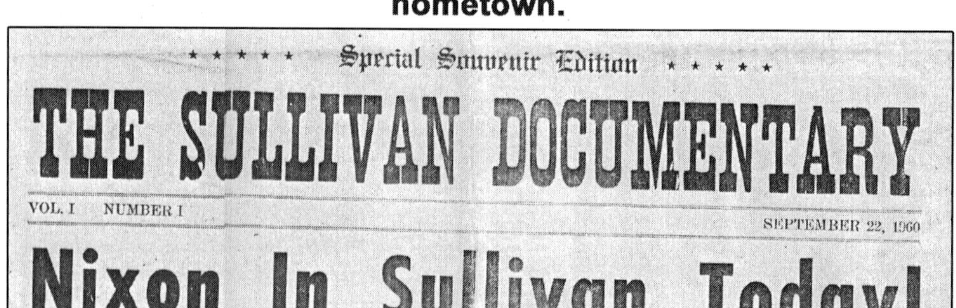

★ ★ ★ ★ ★ Special Souvenir Edition ★ ★ ★ ★ ★

THE SULLIVAN DOCUMENTARY

VOL. I NUMBER I | SEPTEMBER 22, 1960

Nixon In Sullivan Today!

Behind the Scenes Of Sullivan's Day . . .

Why has Richard M. Nixon, Republican candidate for the presidency of the United States, chosen to make a major speech in tiny Sullivan, Illinois, populaton 3,940, at the invitation of the Sullivan Chamber of Commerce?

The inspiring story of how a seemingly unattainable goal has been realized is one of enthusiasm and religious dedication, undaunted in the face of negative reactions, doubts and ridicule.

A plan, born in the minds of Jim Rhodes and Paul Romano, co-chairmen of Sullivan's annual Buffalo Barbecue, was to host both the Democratic and Republican presidential candidates on Buffalo Day for a presentation of their respective party platforms to the people in the heart of America's farm belt.

Rhodes and Romano carried, and sold, their plan to men of the community, and the fever [illegible] The two men teamed with [illegible] Livergood and Bill Stubblefield, and, along with Bruce Shaeffer, executive secretary of the Chamber, began engineering the momentous project.

Now, eight weeks later, Richard M. Nixon's acceptance of the Sullivan invitation, casting him as the first presidential candidate to present a major speech in Sullivan in the city's 115-year history, has made the Political Day a reality.

Program

ARRIVAL TIME, DECATUR AIRPORT, 1:45 P. M.

ARRIVAL TIME, SULLIVAN 2:20 P. M.

PARADE, JACKSON ST. and MAIN ST., 2:20-3:00 P. M.

ARRIVAL TIME SPEAKERS' PLATFORM, 3:00 P. M.

ADDRESS: VICE PRESIDENT RICHARD M. NIXON 3:10 - 3:40 P. M.

BUFFALO BARBECUE BEGINS 3:40 P. M.

Philip H. Best, M. D. will act as master of ceremonies, and Congressman William Springer will introduce Mr. Nixon. Janet Rhodes will serve a buffalo barbecue to Mr. and Mrs. Nixon.

HONORABLE RICHARD M. NIXON

First Visit in History by Vice President

An expected crowd of 50,000 is sharing Sullivan's proudest day today, as Vice-President Richard M. Nixon makes a major address from Wyman Park.

Nixon's appearance and speech marks the first time in the city's 115-year history that a Vice-President of the United States or a candidate for the presidency has graced Sullivan soil.

The Vice-President's party lands at 1:45 p.m. in Decatur. The delegation flys in two Convair aircrafts, one for the Nixon staff and the other for traveling members of the press.

Greeting the Nixons at the airport will be a Sullivan committee headed by Jim Rhodes and Paul Romano, co-chairmen of the annual Buffalo Barbecue.

Also present will be Robert Livergood, acting mayor of Sullivan, James Ralston, president of the Sullivan Chamber of Commerce, [illegible] that set up this historical event.

The group that initially engineered the project, in addition to Romano, Rhodes and Livergood, included Bill Stubblefield and Bruce Shaeffer, executive secretary of the Chamber of Commerce.

After acknowledging whatever sized delegation is on hand at the airport, the Nixon group will join a motor caravan to Sullivan.

Historical Highpoints

A few hours before the Vice President arrived. A huge buffalo head looked small under the gigantic painting of Nixon.

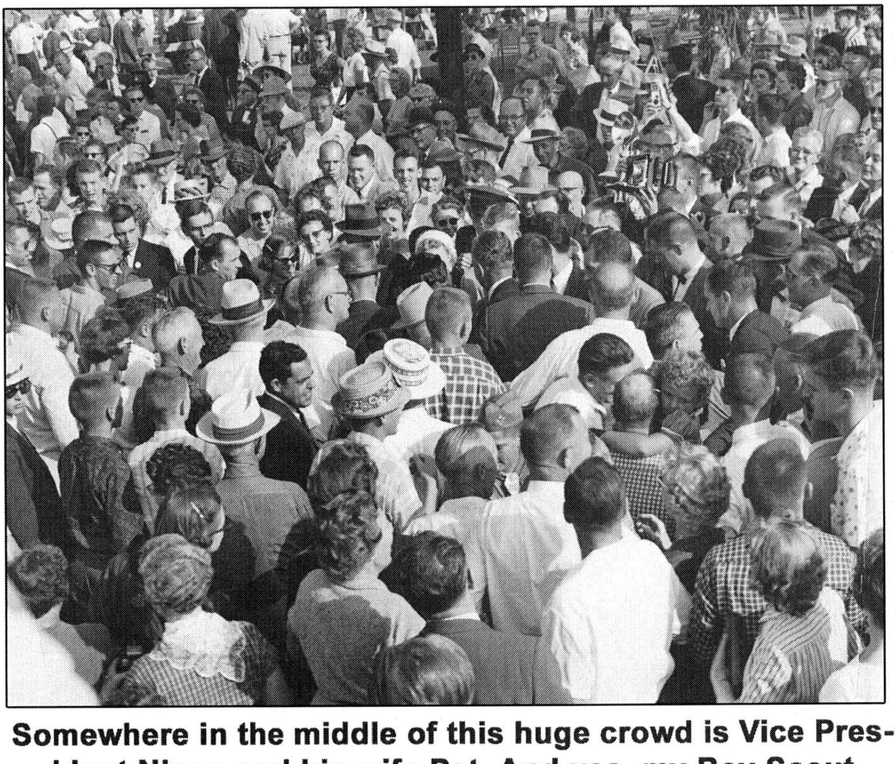

Somewhere in the middle of this huge crowd is Vice President Nixon and his wife Pat. And yes, my Boy Scout troop was in charge of keeping them safe!

Vice President Nixon and his wife Pat arrive at Wyman Park

Local dignitaries on stage with Vice President Nixon

The Vice President addresses the crowd.

NIXONS GO TO A BARBECUE

Politicking on the Prairie

Republican presidential candidate Richard Nixon and his wife Pat invaded Illinois for a series of speeches and appearances and wowed 'em. Here's a pictorial record of his tour of Decatur, Sullivan and Rockford taken by Daily News photographer Edward De Luga.

Everywhere the Nixons went, the crowd went wild. At left, a young lady from Rockford couldn't contain her enthusiasm.

'A Buffalo Burger?'

Highlight of the tour was a buffalo barbecue on the site of one of the Lincoln-Douglas debates of 102 years ago. Nixon (right) had some doubts as he bit into his buffalo burger . . .

'Say, Not Bad . . .'

. . . But doubt turned to enthusiasm and he turned to Samuel Witwer (below), Republican senatorial nominee, who also seemed to be pleased with the taste.

Waves and Whoops

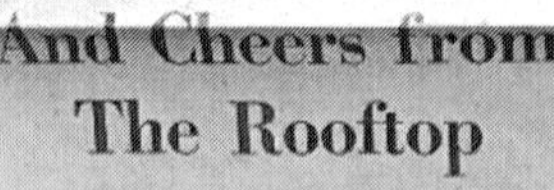

And Cheers from The Rooftop

Nixon's visit got a full page in the Chicago Daily News

Republican presidential candidate Richard Nixon and his wife Pat invaded Illinois for a series of speeches and appearances and wowed 'em. Here's a pictorial record of his tour of Decatur, Sullivan and Rockford taken by Daily News photographer Edward De Luga.

Everywhere the Nixons went, the crowd went wild. At left, a young lady from Rockford couldn't contain her enthusiasm.

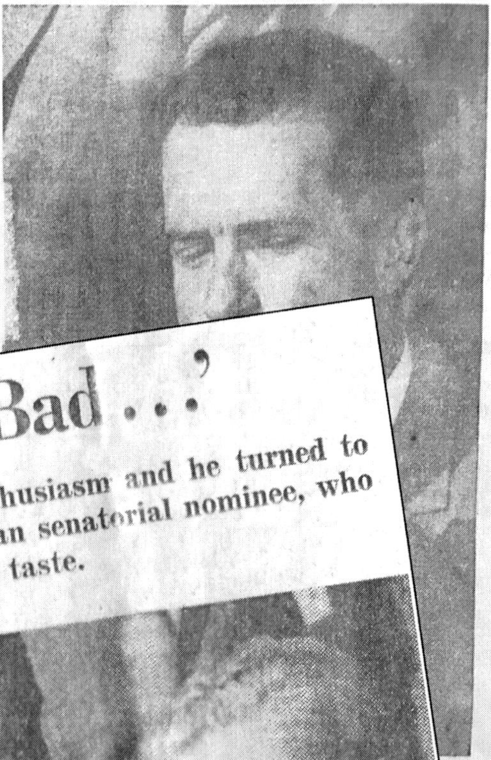

'A Buffalo Burger?'

Highlight of the tour was a buffalo barbecue on the site of one of the Lincoln-Douglas debates of 102 years ago. Nixon (right) had some doubts as he bit into his buffalo burger . . .

'Say, Not Bad . . .'

. . . But doubt turned to enthusiasm and he turned to Samuel Witwer (below), Republican senatorial nominee, who also seemed to be pleased with the taste.

Edward De Luga took the closeup photos of Nixon and the buffalo sandwich for the Chicago Daily News.

The bite that changed my life!

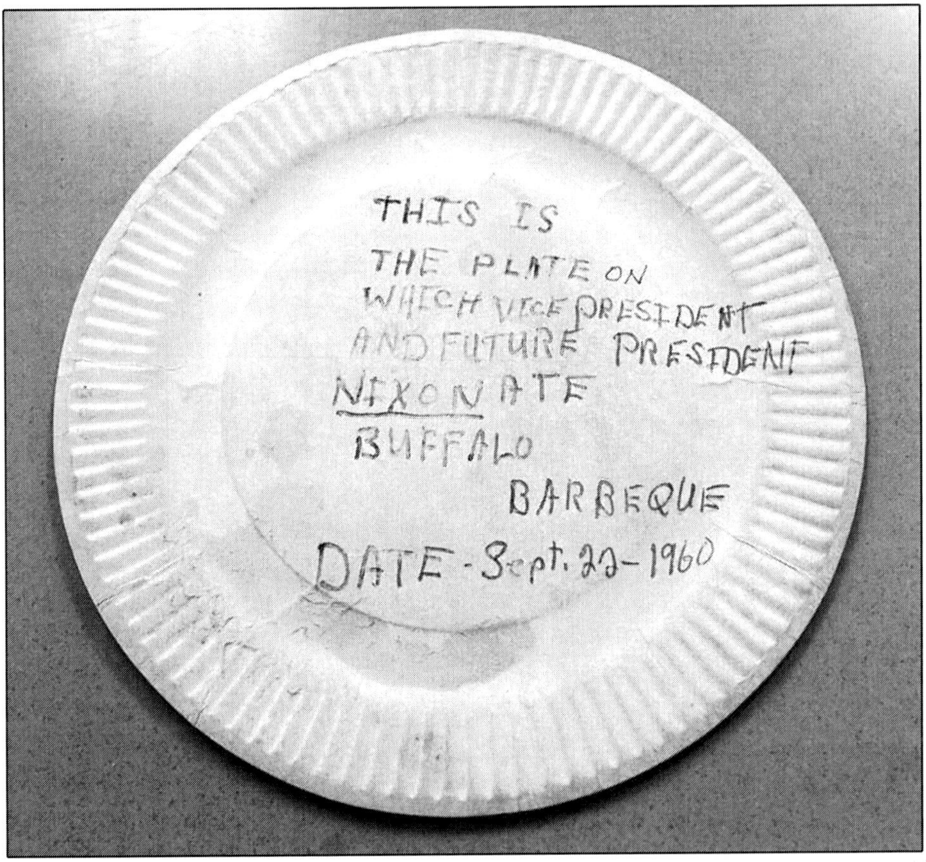

The paper plate Richard Nixon used. I wrote the inscription as soon as I got home from the barbecue.

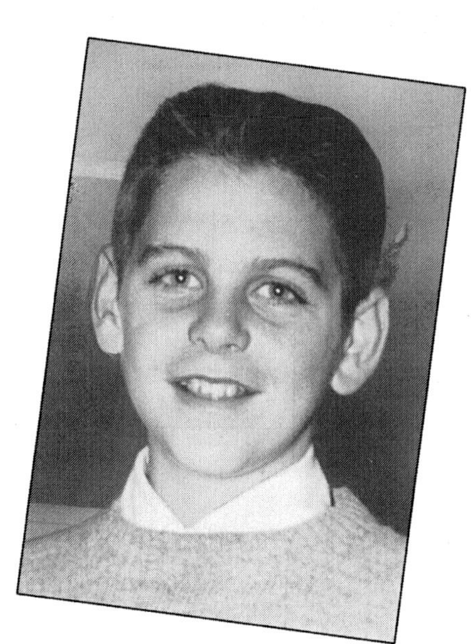

Jane Krows took the photo of me that ran in the Decatur newspaper.

OFFICE OF THE VICE PRESIDENT

WASHINGTON

October 7, 1960

Dear Stephen:

Mrs. Nixon and I were certainly pleased to see so many fine Scouts when we were in Sullivan last month.

Our visit to your friendly town turned out to be one of the most enjoyable stops along our 1960 campaign trail and we wanted to thank you for the part you played in helping to make it so.

With our very best wishes for a successful school year,

Sincerely,

Richard Nixon

Richard Nixon

Mr. Stephen Jenne
1123 West Jackson
Sullivan, Ill

OFFICE OF THE VICE PRESIDENT
WASHINGTON

WASHINGTON D.C. OCT 14 '60
U.S. POSTAGE 04
P.B. METER 171662

Mr. Stephen Jenne
1123 West Jackson
Sullivan, Illinois

"Thank You" letter I received from Vice President Nixon.

Playing football during my Senior year, 1963.

Working on my archaeology job. Summer of 1964 at Lake Shelbyville.

Oct. 1964. With the 1948 Chevy that I still have! My last photo in Sullivan before we moved to Springfield.

College fraternity photo, 1966.

11-27-68 THE DECATUR REVIEW

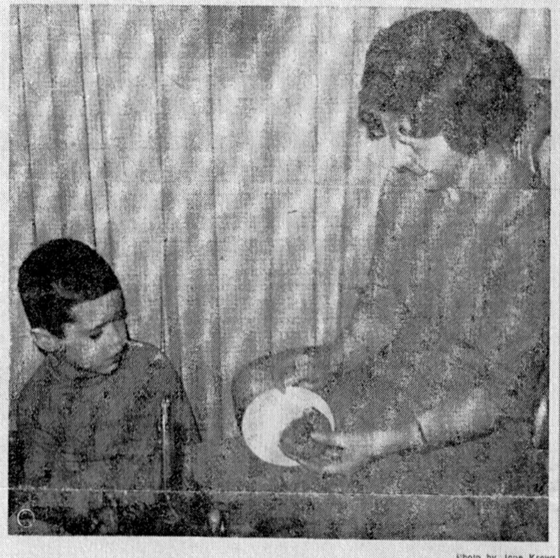

Photo by Jane Krows

Mrs. Loren Jenne and grandson Darren Drake look at sandwich.

Nixon's the One

Sandwich Saved From '60 Campaign

Sullivan (Special)

When Richard M. Nixon campaigned for the presidency in 1960, he and his wife Pat appeared at a buffalo barbeque held at Wyman Park Sullivan.

Before mounting the platform to make his campaign speech, the Nixons were served buffalo barbecue sandwiches.

Nixon toook one good bite out of his sandwich before leaving the picnic table where he was served.

Steve Jenne, son of Mr. and Mrs. Loren Jenne, was a Sullivan High School freshman at that time. He quickly picked up the Nixon sandwich and took it home where it was placed in the family freezer with the hope that Nixon would be elected president in 1960.

Although this did not happen, the sandwich has remained in the Jenne freezer, making the trip from Sullivan to Springfield when they moved a few years ago.

Now that Steve's dream has come true, the sandwich which he was quick enough to salvage that day, is a historic keepsake since Nixon became president-elect.

Steve Jenne is now a senior at Central Missouri University. He has not been home to show off his sandwich since Nixon was elected but Thanksgiving Day his parents took it to a family dinner in Sullivan to show it to nieces, nephews and grandchildren.

Steve spent the holidays in Florida but called his grandmother Mrs. Hallie Carnes in Sullivan to wish her a happy Thanksgiving.

Read Quest in the Review

Decatur Herald newspaper story, as my mother shows off my (then 8 year old) sandwich.

I am officially in the Army. Sept. 15, 1969.
Induction Day, St. Louis.

Who can say they were sworn into the Army by their father? I can!

Visiting with my mom.
Jan. 1970

January 1970. Vietnam here I come.

Photo of me that ran on the front page of the Screaming Eagle 101st Airborne newspaper

My father (seated) with 3 brothers from Sullivan. John, Paul and Don Carnes.

Attempting my first selfie! Somewhere in Vietnam.

During a rare break on Eagle Beach in South Vietnam.

With my friend Wilbur McCoy, reading the local newspaper. They printed this photo in the Moultrie County Newspaper.

Just another day in lovely Vietnam.

I loved our scout dog named Pup.

Wringing the sweat out of my shirt.

My first shave in 3 weeks. On top of Fire Base Gladiator.

More fun times in Vietnam. I couldn't wait to get home!

My 1948 Chevrolet Stylemaster. I still have it!

Ready to take a drive with my dog Tammy.

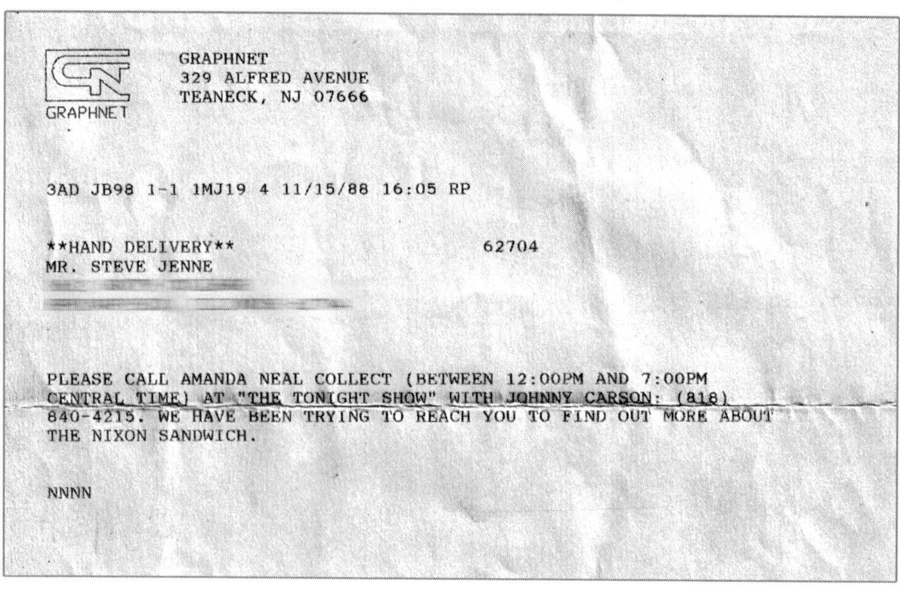

GRAPHNET

GRAPHNET
329 ALFRED AVENUE
TEANECK, NJ 07666

3AD JB98 1-1 1MJ19 4 11/15/88 16:05 RP

HAND DELIVERY 62704
MR. STEVE JENNE

PLEASE CALL AMANDA NEAL COLLECT (BETWEEN 12:00PM AND 7:00PM CENTRAL TIME) AT "THE TONIGHT SHOW" WITH JOHNNY CARSON: (818) 840-4215. WE HAVE BEEN TRYING TO REACH YOU TO FIND OUT MORE ABOUT THE NIXON SANDWICH.

NNNN

Telegram from The Tonight Show after they couldn't reach me by phone.

Heeeeere's Steve with Johnny!

Johnny holding the newspaper article about Nixon's visit

To open...or not to open. Johnny starts to take Nixon's sandwich out of its jar.

Johnny showing Nixon's teeth marks in my sandwich

Trying to be cool as I visit with the King of Late Night.

Johnny takes a bite.

A day in my life that I will never forget.

Johnny tells me to get his sandwich in the freezer as soon as possible.

Steve Martin talks about the paper plate he would give me.

The plate Steve Martin gave me. He wrote, "This is the plate Steve Martin ate a sandwich from before he bomed on the Tonight Show." He misspelled the word bombed.

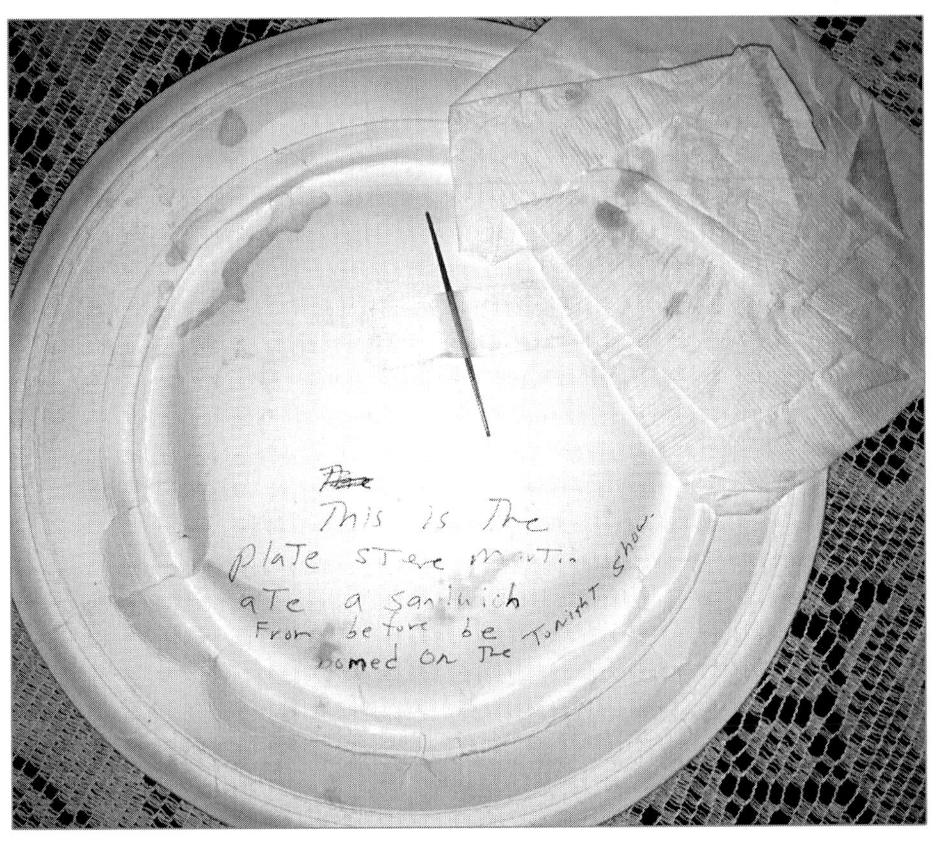

Johnny's used napkin, covered with barbecue sauce, and Steve Martin's plate. The lettuce that had been taped to the plate is long gone.

12-28-88

FROM STEVE JENNE

Dear Vickie,

I asked myself "where do I start?", and my answer was "at the top." You're at the top of my list, so I humbly say "Thank you, thank you, thank you" for your coverage of my recent windfall. We both know that without your article(s), I (we) never would have gone to California! I can't say or do enough (short of falling in debt that is). I also plan to write the editor, and perhaps you'll reap some benefit after all ($?)! It was a fun, fantasy trip which I'll never forget. Please keep in touch!

Sincerely
Steve Jenne

HANSON ENGINEERS INCORPORATED

1525 SOUTH SIXTH STREET ☐ SPRINGFIELD, ILLINOIS 62703-2886 ☐ 217/788-2450
FAX: 217/788-2503

"Thank You" letter I wrote to local reporter Vickie Shaw just after my Tonight Show appearance.

Looking like a real star at the Decatur Celebration.

One of my first fans trying to take in the massive display at the Celebrity Sandwich Man booth at the Decatur Celebration!

Playing pool with LPGA greats Janet Anderson and Judy Dickinson.

LPGA great Sandra Palmer gives me her half-eaten sandwich as a special birthday present.

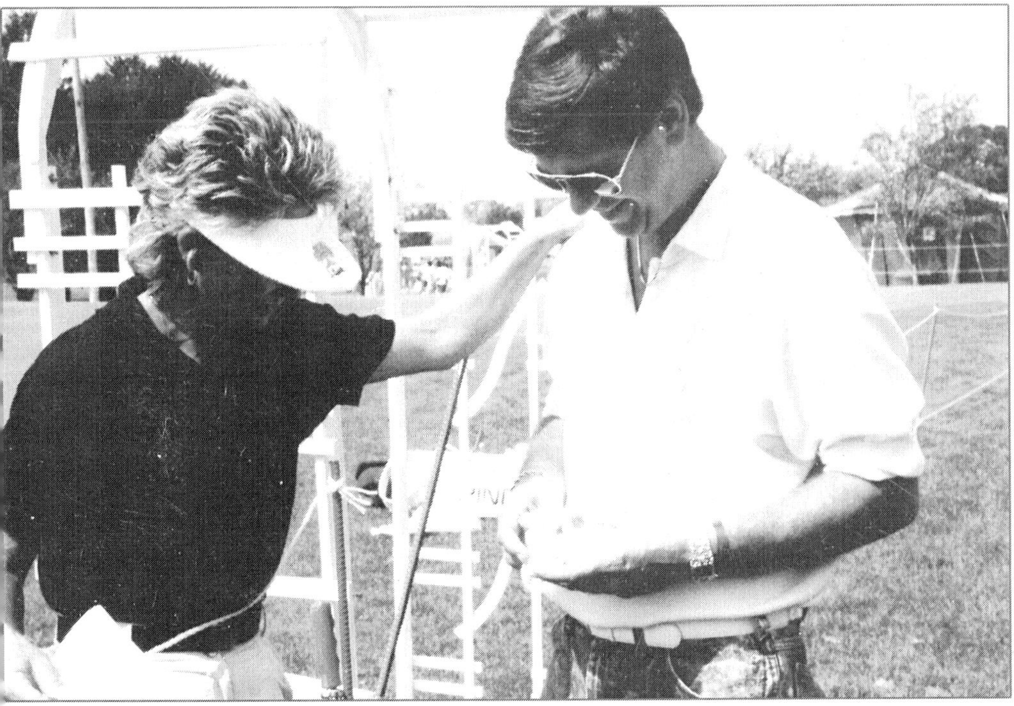

Tiny Tim takes a huge bite of his sandwich, just before it became a part of my collection.

Back before digital cameras. My friend who took the picture only got half of me in the photo!

Hamming it up during another media interview, 1989.

If these sandwiches could talk...what an interesting dinner conversation it would be!

The sandwich that started it all. A close-up during one of the rare times it has been out of the freezer and totally unwrapped.

Heeeere's Johnny's...sandwich!

A tiny portion of Tiny Tim's sandwich. He ate almost the entire thing!

Take a bite...please. Henny Youngman's sandwich.

Yet another media interview and photo shoot.

Featured in a Ripley's Believe It or Not cartoon in 1994.

Page 14-H EXPRESS-NEWS, San Antonio, Texas, Wednesday, May 18, 1994 Recyclable

BELIEVE IT OR NOT

"WALKING TV"

Brian Elliot of Pasadena, Calif., INVENTED A ROBOTIC TELEVISION THAT CAN WALK from ROOM to ROOM!

STEVE JENNE of Springfield, Ill., HAS KEPT A BUFFALO SANDWICH BITTEN INTO BY FORMER U.S. PRESIDENT Richard Nixon — FOR OVER 30 YEARS!

DON'T EAT!

ON 1932, A 10-ft.-WIDE BY 70-MILE-LONG MASS of SEA SNAKES WAS SIGHTED IN THE STRAITS of Malacca!

5-18

With my friend, legendary anthropologist Don Johanson.

With my parents, 1998.

Celebrating my mother's 98th birthday.

Many years after our time in Vietnam, I tracked down my former squad leader Jim Gilreath.

With Lynn Lowder. Lynn has been one of my dearest friends since 1952.

At my dad's funeral. (L-R) Bill Iseminger, Steve Lynch, Steve Jenne, Carl Glazier, Lynn Lowder, Ed Courtright.

With my great friend, Marine Vietnam veteran Ed Courtright.

With my friend and co-writer Scot England.

On the 60th anniversary of the Nixon visit. Yes, we are both a little older, but the sandwich and I are both still here!

The Nixon sandwich, age 60, still inside the original Musselman's Applesauce jar.

First Class. As we got off the plane, one of the stewardesses said, "I am so sorry about that. That lady didn't want to sit by someone who had fought in Vietnam." I shook my head, "You have got to be kidding."

When I walked into the airport, Mom and Dad were there to meet me. We had a tearful reunion. Then I had another rude awakening. As we went outside, I was met by protesters shouting, "Baby killer!" That was followed by someone spitting at me. It was quite the homecoming.

Before we left Chicago, my parents treated me to a steak dinner. I consumed it in no time. Mother was shocked at how fast I finished my meal. That night, Dad took me to a place called the Millionaires Club. (You didn't have to be a millionaire to go there though.) It was just a nice restaurant, where Dad often went. I was still in my uniform, but as soon as we got to the door, the maître'd stopped us and loudly announced, "You must have a coat and tie to come in. That uniform is not allowed." My Dad said, "That's ridiculous."

That night, Dad and I went out for drinks and I said, "I am officially an unemployed, college graduate, combat veteran." When I finally got home to Springfield, I went out to a place called The Warehouse. It had great steaks and good entertainment. I decided to see if the reaction to a Vietnam vet was different in Springfield than it was in Chicago, so I wore my uniform. After all, I still had no civilian clothes that I could fit into.

The place was packed, but I found a table for four and sat down by myself…and I stayed by myself. No one came near me. The waitresses wouldn't even wait on me. After a little bit, another waitress finally came over to me. I ordered a Scotch and water and she said, "This is on the gentleman over there." She pointed at a man across the room. He walked over and said, "I'm a Vietnam vet too." He sat down and we visited. I said, "Man, this sucks. I can't believe people hate the guys who we're trying to protect." He answered, "You'll get used to it."

But I never did get used to it…as similar incidents occurred for many years. A few days later, a bank teller I had known since I was a kid growing up in Sullivan, laughed at me and said, "What happened to you? You look like hell!" True, I had lost a lot of weight (I only weighed 139 lbs.) and was admittedly gaunt and probably did not look like I "fit in" with her crowd anymore. I would still wear my Army field jacket, replete with patches I had earned, and folks would either quickly glance the other way or make some sort of snide comment about my service.

In the photo section of this book, I've included a few of my pictures from Vietnam. These were the ones I was allowed to bring home . . . pictures that were not considered "contraband" by MPs assigned to inspect everything that GIs possessed before we returned to the states. As I look at the pictures, I see how dirty and haggard I looked, as did the rest of my squad; unshaven, clad in fatigues we hadn't changed in 3 weeks, gaunt, with that 1,000 yard stare, all of us. I looked old. We all looked old, older than we really were. Vietnam did that to us.

Shortly after I came home, so did my friend Wilbur McCoy. We had made a vow while in Vietnam to get together again back in Sullivan, Illinois, when we were both back home. We kept that vow, and our first reunion was at a local bar. Some drunk guy made a negative comment about our "attire", which included the Screaming Eagle patch of the 101st Airborne we were both wearing. I learned early on that one should NEVER say anything bad about our country to Wilbur. He was one of the nicest guys in the world, if he liked you. But he was also one of the toughest guys I have ever known, and you did not want to cross him. Slugging back long-necks and shooting pool were the norm for us, while cussing and discussing some of our more memorable missions. It felt good to spend time with someone you served with and someone you knew would understand anything and everything we talked about. Wilbur McCoy passed away on May 23, 2002. Rest in Honored Peace, Wilbur. I will NEVER forget you!

While I was in Vietnam, my Dad was transferred from Springfield to Chicago. My parents kept our house in Springfield, while he rented a home in Downers Grove. Dad's plane came in handy, as he could fly home on weekends instead of making the long drive. When I returned to Springfield after serving my country, I really didn't want to do anything. I didn't know what my future held.

As I thought about my next move, I heard a song by The Drifters called "Up on the Roof." I listened to the lyrics, "When this ol' world starts getting you down..." I thought, "Maybe I could get a better look at my future if I went up on the roof." So I did! I climbed up the TV antenna and sat on the roof, accompanied by a portable radio, a 6-pack of beer, and a pack of cigarettes. I still have my cigarette lighter from Vietnam.

Dutch Miller, a Vice President of Hanson Engineers, was our neighbor across the street. Hanson did structural, transportation and environmental engineering and foundations. He saw me up on the roof, walked over, and yelled up, "Hey, Steve! Would you like to come to work for us?" I flatly said, "No." But for some reason, Dutch felt I would be an asset to their company. Over the next few weeks, he asked me a couple more times if I would come in for an interview. I finally relented, and I'm glad that I did.

In November 1971, they hired me to work in their soils lab. I enjoyed the job and I enjoyed the people I worked with, but I felt that I could do more. I went to Dutch and told him I was going to quit. He passed the word to the company vice president Lee Dondanville, and Lee immediately called me into his office. Lee said that he knew I had a degree in Mass Media, Radio and TV, and he wanted me to be in charge of their new Public Relations department. As part of my job as Communications Coordinator, I read and proof-read thousands of engineering reports. I found out that many engineers were amazing at their jobs, but spelling for some (but not all) was not a strong point.

In October 1978, I bought my first house. It was a dilapidated, run-down home in a nice, quiet neighborhood in the middle of Springfield. Dad, now retired, and I renovated the old house. I duplexed it and within 13 months of my purchase, I had my first renter. I was able to completely pay off the house in no time.

Life was good in Springfield. I loved my job, and I also took on a second one. My lawn mower had quit on me and I took it to Dad because he excelled in lawn mower repair. I watched him fix it and I was surprised at how easy he made it look. Dad said, "You'd be surprised at how many people can't fix their lawn mower." That inspired me to get into the lawn mower repair business.

I bought lawn mower books and repair manuals. I learned everything I could about Briggs & Stratton and Tecumseh engines. If there was something I couldn't figure out, I'd call Dad and he would always be able to fix anything that I couldn't. I soon found myself with a booming part-time repair business. I also bought old or broken mowers, repaired them in my basement, and then resold them.

I invested the money I made from my lawn mower repairs into another hobby. I bought audio equipment including speakers, amps, microphones, turntables and tape players, and I started my own DJ service. I had business cards printed, and I took my show on the road. I ended up getting $500 a night to play my music at wedding receptions or birthday parties.

I also used my DJ talents when I served on the committee for the Vietnam Veterans Memorial in Springfield, Illinois. The music I had put together was exactly what my Vietnam vet buddies liked to hear.

Because of my DJ experience and also thanks to my knowledge of late ‘60s and early ‘70s Vietnam era music, I was asked to serve as emcee at the “Delta to the DMZ” dance in Washington, D.C. The event was a fundraiser for the Vietnam Veterans Nurses Memorial that would be erected in Washington, D.C.

Dean Bricker, who worked with me at Hanson Engineers, helped me DJ the event in D.C. After we checked into our hotel, I went down to check out the ballroom. It was locked, with a guard outside the door, who told me I couldn’t go in without proper credentials. I said, “Well if you don’t let me in, you’re not going to have any entertainment tonight.” He got on his walkie-talkie and found someone to get me in, this time with credentials.

During a private party after the dance, I was able to meet a number of celebrities. The most memorable one to me was actress Dana Delany. Dana portrayed Vietnam nurse Diane Carlson Evans on the hit TV series "China Beach".

I loved being a DJ…until the night that someone broke into my van and stole every piece of equipment that I had! It was all gone. The police were never able to recover anything, so I was immediately out of the deejay business.

CHAPTER SIX – HERE'S JOHNNY!

1988 was an election year. George H.W. Bush was running against Michael Dukakis to see who would succeed Ronald Reagan as President. Vicki Shaw, a local newspaper reporter, was going through old files, looking for story ideas, when she ran across the original 1960 article about me taking Richard Nixon's sandwich. She wondered if there was any way I could still have the presidential artifact.

After tracking me down at my new home in Springfield, and after being totally amazed that yes, I did have the now 28 year-old sandwich, Vicki decided to write a follow up article.

In our phone interview, she explained that she covered the Mattoon bureau of the *Decatur Herald and Review* newspaper. Two days later, the article appeared in the paper's Saturday edition. The story's headline read, "28 years later, Nixon's bite lingers on."

As I went to the store to buy a couple extra copies of the paper, I had no idea what was going to hit me less than 48 hours later!

On October 24th, 1988, the Associated Press picked up the story on their national wires. That means my story went out to EVERY newspaper, radio and TV station in the world! My life was about to change drastically.

News of "my Nixon sandwich" went around the globe overnight. My first hint that the story was "going viral" was at 5 a.m. the morning after the article appeared in the Decatur paper. I received a call from radio station WLS in Chicago. The DJs wanted to talk to me for their "morning drive" segment.

Then I did a live interview with WMAQ radio in Chicago. They played that interview another four times throughout the day. As soon as the live interview was over, I got another call, and then another, and another. The calls went on incessantly over the course of several weeks.

I got calls to do interviews from New York to San Francisco, and from Hawaii to Canada. I even got a call from a reporter in London, England, and then I did an interview with the British Broadcasting Company, out of Belfast, Ireland!

When I was completely booked with interviews, my Mom filled in for me. She handled each radio and newspaper interview like a true pro. Over the next month, Mom would do interviews with radio stations, from San Jose, California to Washington, D.C.

In the October 24, 1988 edition of the Chicago Tribune, I was listed in their "Newsmakers" column. In the article, my Mother was quoted as saying, "I think the sandwich has survived better than Nixon." It was a line she originally said to Vicki Shaw for the Decatur newspaper.

That same day, the story also appeared in the USA Today newspaper. I tried my best to keep up with all the interview requests, but I didn't want to take off from my job; so I did a number of interviews early in the morning before I went in to work. When I got home that evening, my answering machine was completely full with more interview requests.

I think this would be a good place to tell you that I have never looked for any publicity. I wasn't a "publicity nut". I never contacted any TV or radio stations; I didn't have a publicist or agent whose job was to get me attention; I never sought out interviews…but I never turned any down either. I said "yes" to every request I received. It seemed that each interview would lead to another. One story here would reach another news outlet there, and they would want to do their own interview with me.

I never really got tired of it, and I enjoyed answering the same questions over and over. Some of the most often asked questions were:

Why did you take the sandwich?

Why did you save it all these years?

Would you ever sell it?

Did you ever hear from President Nixon?

No, Richard Nixon never called me, and I never expected him to. But I seemed to hear from almost everyone in the world...except him!

After each radio and television interview and after each newspaper story was published, when at all possible, I always made a point to write a "Thank You" note to each reporter. I also wrote Letters to the Editor to thank each newspaper for covering me.

On October 25, 1988, the executive producer of the David Letterman TV show called to talk about me possibly being on the show. After our initial conversation, they never called back. I am so glad they didn't, because less than a month later, I was contacted by the (much higher rated and much more iconic) "Tonight Show with Johnny Carson!"

On November 16, as I thumbed through my mail, seeing what bills I had received that day, I saw an envelope that read "Airborne Express: Extremely Urgent Material Enclosed." I thought it was junk mail and I didn't bother opening it until later that night. When I finally got around to opening it, I found an express telegram from The Tonight Show. It was a request that I call them immediately.

When I finally made the call, Amanda Neal, who was the assistant to the Executive Producer of the show, sounded more excited than I was. She yelled, “Oh, Mr. Jenne, we’ve been trying to reach you!” Amanda explained that my story had caught her attention as she read an article about me in the USA Today newspaper.

Amanda transferred me to Debbie Vickers, a producer with the show. Debbie asked me if I could take time off from work to fly out to California. She also asked if I could bring the Nixon sandwich. As we talked, I answered every question she asked with, “Yes, I can.” The entire time I was thinking, “I will do whatever I have to do get on that show!” I couldn’t believe they were interested, but I didn’t want to blow my big chance!

The next day, I went to work and told some co-workers, “They want me on the Tonight Show.” Even though it wasn’t a done deal, I couldn’t keep it a secret. It was just too exciting. It didn’t take long for word to get around, and the local Springfield newspaper ran a short story about me possibly being on the show.

With each day that passed, and with each new question of “Hey, Steve have you heard from Johnny yet?”, the more nervous I got. I didn’t want to look like a fool if the show ended up passing on me.

But on November 30th, much to my relief, I got the official word that I was going to be a guest on the show! They told me the taping date would be in mid-December.

As the Carson show date approached, the producers called me 10 to 15 times. It seemed every day they always had one thing or another that they needed to finalize. They sent me a 20 page contract, full of “legalese”. It stated they would do a major background check on me. I didn’t care. I knew the worst thing they’d find on me was a half-eaten 28 year-old sandwich in my freezer.

The show also had a unique request. In addition to bringing my Nixon sandwich, they also wanted me to bring along some fresh buffalo meat. They didn’t tell me why they wanted it, but I figured they were going to use it for some kind of gag for Johnny.

I contacted Tony Turasky of Turasky’s Catering Service in Springfield and he knew of a place in Seward, Illinois that had buffalo meat. When I called them, they said they would be honored to send me some for Johnny.

As we went back and forth in the weeks before the show, I kept praying that I would be on during a night when Johnny was there. At the time, it seemed that Johnny was gone almost as much as he was on the show. During his absences, the show always had guest hosts. But I didn’t want a guest host. I wanted The King!

Just before the taping, I received word that yes, Johnny would indeed be there. For younger folks who might have missed out on Johnny Carson, it is hard to explain how big and how popular he was. This was back before we had 500 channels of nothing to watch. Back then, we had 3 to 5 channels and at 10:30 every night, almost everyone in the country tuned in to watch The Tonight Show.

Johnny was very funny. But he was known for his interviews with TV and movie stars. All of the biggest show biz legends went on his show. But Johnny was at his best when he had "regular people" on the show. He was great with someone whose claim to fame was that they were 110 years old, and he was also great with kids. He treated those people just like he treated all the rich and famous stars he had on. But the producers of the show called the guests who weren't in show business "civilians." They were regular folks who Johnny liked to recognize and make famous for a few minutes. I was considered a civilian.

The show gave me the choice of a first class, round trip plane ticket and travel alone, or I could take a guest and travel by coach. I chose the latter and took a lady friend with me.

Just before we flew to California, I received a nice card from Vicki Shaw. Vicki was the newspaper reporter who wrote the updated article earlier that year that led to my "overnight fame". Vicki said she was proud of me and she wished me well on my appearance. I still have her card.

I also still have the TV Guide from that week. The issue came out just before I left to tape the show. When I got it, I immediately turned to the day of my Carson show. I felt like I had stepped into the Twilight Zone when I read, "December 14, 1988 – Johnny Carson Show/Guests: Steve Martin, Nixon fan Steve Jenne"! When I found out that Steve Martin was also going to be on the show, I was overjoyed. Steve had always been one of my favorites.

On the day of our flight, a limousine picked us up at my house and took us to the Springfield airport, where we were met by local newspaper and TV reporters. After a few more interviews, we stepped onto a local commuter turbo-prop plane that would fly us to Chicago O'Hare Airport, where we'd take a much bigger plane to California.

As I looked out the plane window, I silently thought, "I hope I won't be visibly nervous. I hope Johnny doesn't make me look like a fool." I knew this was the big time, and it was hard not to be nervous.

When we landed in Los Angeles, we saw a man in the baggage claim area, holding a big sign that read "S. Jenne". He introduced himself as our chauffeur, and drove us to the Sheraton Universal Hotel. It was a very nice hotel that was billed as "Where the Stars Stay".

The Carson show didn't mind spending money. They could have flown us straight in on the day of the taping and flown us right back to Illinois. But instead, they brought us there on Monday and would pay for all of our stay through Thursday. The actual show taping was Wednesday afternoon.

As we walked into the hotel lobby, a rep from the Carson show greeted us. She explained that she would be back in the morning to interview me. From that interview, they would make a script that Johnny Carson would use as an outline for our conversation on his show.

After my interview with the show rep, my guest and I had the rest of the day and the following day and night to ourselves. I wanted to enjoy as much of my trip as I could, but I found myself almost constantly concerned about my Nixon sandwich. When we arrived in Los Angeles, I immediately took the cooler that held my prized possession to the hotel kitchen. I watched as a worker carefully sat it inside their large freezer. I made sure they put a big sign on my cooler so no one would throw it away. Unfortunately, they put the cooler that held my sandwich next to some fish. When I pulled the cooler from the freezer, I said, "Oh my gosh! It smells like fish!" Luckily the smell didn't get inside the cooler.

We spent a lot of our free time sunning and relaxing out by the hotel pool. I also spent some time in and around the hotel lounge. That's where I happened to run into actor Telly

Savalas. At the time, Telly was known for his very popular "Kojak" TV series. He was also known for his bald head and his love for lollipops. Telly's popular catch phrase was "Who loves ya, baby?" On the afternoon before my taping, Telly was having a drink, relaxing and watching TV in the lounge. He had control of the television remote control. I thought, "Telly is in charge of the telly."

I introduced myself to him and he asked why I was appearing on the Tonight Show. As I tried to explain "my Tonight Show worthiness", he started laughing. He couldn't believe it. The more he thought about it, the louder he laughed. If Telly were alive today, he'd still be laughing! He just kept shaking his head, and all the time I was very much enjoying the drinks that Telly and I shared together.

On the day of the show, our limo driver wheeled us into the NBC lot. The guard at the gate said, "Yes, indeed, Steve Jenne is on the VIP list", as he checked off our names and signaled the limo through. I was surprised to see that Johnny Carson did not have the Number 1 reserved parking spot. That belonged to consumer advocate David Horowitz.

Once inside, we were given a tour of the set and the other nearby studios. We saw the big wheel for The Wheel of Fortune. We walked past Vanna White's dressing room, but didn't see Vanna.

Then they took me to the makeup salon, which reminded me of an expensive barbershop. A gorgeous young lady was assigned to do my makeup. I was impressed that I could easily make her laugh as I shared some quips about the reason I was on the show.

When I was in the makeup chair, someone popped in the door, and said, “Oh, excuse me. I’ll be back for mine later.” I didn’t catch a glimpse of him, but the makeup woman casually said, “Oh, that was Johnny.” He didn’t like to talk to guests before the show. He wanted everything to be very spontaneous on the air. I also didn’t meet his sidekick and show M.C. Ed McMahon until we shook hands as I walked onto the set. I also never got to see Ed or Johnny after the show.

After getting my makeup on, they took us to my own private dressing room. It had a full bathroom and shower, table, chairs, sofa and TV sets. The outside of the door had a sign with my name and “The Tonight Show” logo. As I read “Steve Jenne”, I told myself, “This is really happening!”

Soon there was a knock on my door. It was the show’s producer, Fred de Cordova, whom I instantly recognized. Johnny often poked fun at Fred on the show. Mr. de Cordova smiled as he welcomed me. He shook my hand and genuinely made me feel comfortable. Fred told me, “Just have fun and be yourself.”

Fred gave me a script that included the questions Johnny would ask…and it also included the answers I was to give. The script was eight pages long. As I thumbed through it, I realized that during our "ad-libbed" interview, Johnny wanted to know everything I was going to say before I said it. He knew my answers before he asked the questions. But once we started with the actual show, Johnny didn't stick to the script at all. He basically ignored the script, and he truly ad-libbed most of our conversation. I still have my original script from the show.

Mr. de Cordova explained that I would be the first guest of the night. Yes, fans of Steve Martin had to sit through Steve Jenne before they got to see him! Fred then asked if I would like a drink. My guest and I both accepted.

From that moment, it seemed like the barmaid was knocking on our door every ten minutes and each time, I enjoyed the Scotch and water she made for me. They really encouraged me to imbibe as much as I wanted. However, I thought I might end up getting too loose, so I finally had to shut myself off. I thought, "I have a big show to do, and I don't want to fall on my face in front of Johnny!"

As the start time neared, I was ushered into the "Green Room". That's a room (surprisingly not green at all) where all the guests wait for their time to go on. My guest chose to stay with me and watch the show from backstage in the "Green Room," instead of from the audience.

We could watch the live feed of the show on a TV monitor, while we could hear the audience laughter and all the music just outside the door. When Doc Severinsen's band kicked off the show's theme song, I had to actually pinch myself. Then I couldn't believe my ears as I heard Ed McMahon announce me as a show guest! He billed me as "Nixon Sandwich Saver, Steve Jenne". I shook my head in total disbelief when I heard Ed say the magical words, "Heeeeere's Johnny!"

I tried to stay calm as I told myself, "Don't try to outdo Johnny. He is the star. Just be yourself." I didn't have to worry about "outdoing Johnny"! Whatever little quip I would come up with, he would always top mine.

After Johnny finished his monologue, he talked about the guests who would be on the show. As he described me saving the sandwich, the crowd groaned. Johnny then said, "That's the kind of man we want on our show!" As they went to the first break, I was escorted to an area just beyond the large curtained backdrop to the show. Doc Severinsen and his band were walking by, and a member of the band stopped and asked me, "You're from Sullivan, Illinois? I'm from Tuscola!" Tuscola is about 30 miles from my hometown. That quick conversation seemed to calm my nerves a little bit.

Since it was a show around the holidays, for the first five or ten minutes after the monologue, Johnny read Christmas cards from kids. My Mother who was watching at home in Illinois, kept saying, "Let's get this over with! I'm getting sick of hearing these cards from kids!"

Leading up to the show, I was concerned that Johnny might make fun of me. I was also worried he would make fun of my small hometown of Sullivan, Illinois. I shared those thoughts with Guy Little Jr., who owned the Little Theatre on the Square in Sullivan. Guy wrote me a lovely letter that boosted my confidence. I actually took that letter with me to Hollywood and I had it in my vest pocket as I sat with Johnny!

When his Christmas card segment was finally over, Johnny mentioned all the guests on the show. Again, I thought it was so funny that I was the first guest of the night. The big star Steve Martin, who was promoting his new movie "Dirty Rotten Scoundrels" would have to wait until I was off! And actress Helen Shaver was the last guest on the show. The following night, the big star on the show was Bob Hope. It would have been great to meet Bob, but I was more than satisfied by meeting Johnny, Ed, Doc and Steve Martin.

I always wore glasses. But I didn't really like the way I looked with glasses. So just before Johnny started reading my introduction, I took my glasses off and put them in my sport coat pocket. Johnny's intro was almost word for word as was written in our script. But he made it sound like he was making it up as he went. Yes, he was a pro.

As Johnny finished my introduction, I stepped from behind the curtain and walked onstage. Johnny shook my hand and then Ed McMahon greeted me. It was the first time

I had said a word to either one of them. I couldn't see any of the audience; the lights were too bright, so I couldn't tell how many people were in the audience. Of course, my glasses in my coat pocket didn't help my eyesight any!

I gingerly placed the glass jar with the still-frozen Nixon sandwich on Johnny's desk. I sat the jar right next to Johnny's favorite coffee cup, and explained the complete history of the sandwich. I also showed him the little paper plate on which the sandwich had been placed. Johnny read out loud the inscription I wrote, "This is the plate on which Vice President and future President Nixon ate at the buffalo barbeque. September 22, 1960." Then he said, "You could probably sell this to some museum." Then he deadpanned, "A very pathetic museum."

Over the years, I've often been asked if I would sell the sandwich to a museum or collector. I really haven't seriously thought about it. I might consider donating it to the Nixon library…if they promised to display it in a refrigerated case.

During our conversation, Ed McMahon gave a number of his hearty laughs and Johnny did a number of his famous eye rolls and double takes. But he never made me feel like he was making fun of me. He acted like he was truly enjoying our visit. I know I was.

Johnny opened the jar and was going to take the entire sandwich out, but he chose to leave it inside as he held it up for a close-up camera shot. When he said, "People can actually see the teeth prints right here," the audience just went crazy. Johnny also held up a newspaper that had a large photo of Nixon eating the sandwich.

I had never been on TV before, and this was BIG TIME TV! But I was surprisingly calm and comfortable. Johnny was great at making his guests feel comfortable, and of course the Scotch that his staff had served me before the show also didn't hurt.

As planned, the show's chef had prepared some of the fresh buffalo barbecue I had brought from Illinois. They had a warm sandwich sitting next to Johnny's desk. After taking a large bite, Johnny playfully offered me the remaining part of his meal, to which I quickly agreed!

Johnny said the barbecue was tasty and then wiped some barbecue sauce from his mouth with a couple napkins. As Johnny looked for a place to dispose of the napkins, I chimed in that I would take them. He quipped, "Oh, so you want the napkin too?" As he handed them to me, he gave one last eye roll while the audience howled with laughter.

As he started to thank me for coming, Johnny asked, "You're really not going to save this are you?" When I answered, "Watch me!" Johnny doubled over his desk in delight. I thought, "I made Johnny Carson laugh! How cool is this?"

With that, I started to leave the stage with two partially eaten sandwiches, Nixon's and Carson's, along with the paper plate Nixon had used, and Johnny's napkins. I shook Johnny's hand and stuffed his napkins into my sport coat pocket. As I walked toward the curtain, there was a thunderous roar of laughter and applause from the crowd, as well as the staff backstage.

When I walked backstage as the show went to break, everyone was just going crazy! People started running over, slapping me on the back, congratulating me. One person after another came to shake my hand and say what a great job I did. I could still hear the audience laughing and cheering. It made me feel good.

To be honest, while I was out there on the set, I had no idea how I was doing. It was all a whirlwind and I could barely remember a word I said. But backstage, the entire crew was just showering me with love. Even the lady who had been serving me all the drinks was laughing! Then the floor director came running up to me and said, "Mr. Jenne! Steve Martin would like to meet you!" I couldn't believe it, as I was being escorted to Steve's dressing room. He was just minutes away from going on the show, but he wanted to show me what he was going to do.

He explained that he had just finished eating a chicken salad sandwich and that I had "given him an inspiration". Before he went out to Johnny, Steve wanted to run his "inspiration" by me first! He planned to walk out to meet Johnny as he carried a paper plate. He had taped a piece of lettuce and a toothpick to the plate, and had written on the plate, "This is the plate on which Steve Martin ate a chicken sandwich before he bombed on The Tonight Show!" (He actually misspelled 'bombed" and wrote it as "bomed".)

As he got ready to leave his dressing room, Steve said he wanted me to have the plate after he showed it to Johnny. After his segment, during a commercial break, I was given the plate...which I still have today.

I'm sure the show's producers had scripted all of Steve's appearance and interview, just like they had with me. But he threw that entire script out the window when I gave him the "inspiration" for his segment. I'm also sure that his improvisation turned out much better than the original script!

My guest was able to say hello to Steve Martin and actress Helen Shaver backstage after the show. But she never got to meet Johnny or Ed McMahon. You can still see my appearance on YouTube. Just do a search for "Johnny Carson Analyzes Richard Nixon's Half Eaten Sandwich."

After the taping, before we left my dressing room, there was one person I wanted to call first. That person was Vicki Shaw, the Decatur, Illinois newspaper reporter whose story led me to where I was standing at the NBC studios in Hollywood!

I haven't had any contact with Vicki for the past 30 years, but I thought this book would give me a good reason to try to find her again. Today, she is Vicki Shaw Woodard. After writing for the *Decatur Herald and Review* for four years, she worked the next 25 years doing public relations at Eastern Illinois University. These are some of her memories of the crazy time she put me through:

"I started working for the Mattoon bureau of the *Decatur Herald* in 1988, just a short time before Steve Jenne's sandwich story fell into my lap.

One of our editors in the Decatur office was going through the archives, looking for any political related story that might be of interest. They ran across the original, small story about Steve and the Nixon sandwich. They tossed out the idea to all the reporters and everyone passed on it. They all thought it was a cute story, but no one wanted to do it. It went down the entire line of everyone until it got to the low person on the totem pole…me!

I thought it would be a nice human interest and "look back" piece. So I tracked Steve down, and I was totally shocked that he still had the sandwich!

I did my interviews with Steve over the phone, but we did meet in person one time. We met in Sullivan, and I took a photo of him so we would have an updated picture of him for the paper. That was the one and only time we met in person and believe it or not, I never got to see the sandwich "in person" or up close.

As soon as the newspaper printed my story on Steve, they submitted it to the Associated Press, and almost instantly, it was picked up, not only across the U.S., but also in different countries around the world. I had no idea that it would go as far as it did.

When I found out he was going to be on The Tonight Show, I was very happy for him. The story was Steve's; I was just the storyteller. But I was very proud that my efforts contributed to helping him get there, and that made me feel good. It also gave me an extra boost of confidence in my ability, and it gave me a feeling that I was making a difference in someone's life.

All of my co-workers and the other reporters couldn't believe it when they found out that Steve was going to be on the Johnny Carson Show. They knew that it was my story that had kind of led to everything and they knew they had all turned it down! My partner in the Mattoon bureau, Jeff Raymond said, 'Shoot! I could have done that one!'

The night The Tonight Show aired, the entire newspaper staff in Decatur gathered around the TV in the newsroom. When Steve came on, everything came to a stop as everyone watched the show. The moment Steve walked off after his interview with Johnny, the whole staff just burst into applause.

As soon as his taping with Johnny Carson was over, Steve phoned me. He said, 'Vicki, I'm calling you from my personal dressing room!' He couldn't talk long, but he tried to give me all the details he could. I thought it was so nice of him to call me while he was still there in the studio.

Steve also sent me a couple "Thank You" notes that I have kept all these years. He also sent a Letter to the Editor of the Decatur paper, thanking me publicly. He was very kind. He was a really fun, interesting and nice guy to get to know." - Vicki Shaw Woodard

The Tonight Show was taped around 3:00 in the afternoon, hours before its 10:30 p.m. central time airing. After we said goodbye to everyone at the show, we decided to celebrate my appearance by going out to a nice dinner.

We still had access to our limousine, so I asked our driver to take us to a very fancy, up-scale restaurant. While we enjoyed our meal, a few of the other patrons came over to me and wanted to say hello. I couldn't fathom how they knew me, but they explained they had been in the audience during the taping. One of them kept looking up at my forehead and I realized I still had my TV makeup on. It had all caked up, but my guest said that she thought I looked just fine.

After dinner, along with my Nixon and Carson sandwiches, we were chauffeured back to our hotel. That night, we watched The Tonight Show on the TV in our hotel room. I actually thought I had done a pretty good job.

The next day, we were driven to the airport, where we caught a short flight to Santa Barbara. I rented a car there, and we drove northeast to Solvang. (Solvang is Danish for "Valley of the Sun.") It was the town where I had first started the first grade back in the early 1950s. We stayed with an old family friend named Flossie Jensen, who treated and fed us like royalty.

As we toured Solvang, I was again surprised by several people who said they recognized me from the show the night before. The next day, we drove back to Santa Barbara and after one more night in California, we boarded our plane for our return flight home.

When we got off the plane in Springfield, I was met again by a group of TV, radio and newspaper reporters. They all treated me like a real celebrity…even though I knew I wasn't one. On the local news that night, they named the story, "A Star Returns". On my first day back at work, all of my co-workers shook my hand, slapped my back and said, "You did a great job, Steve!"

As I was putting this book together, I asked my sister Lynette how she felt about my being on The Tonight Show, and here are some of her thoughts:

"I was not surprised that Stephen kept the sandwich all these years. I know it was just something fun for him. It was fun for our entire family. But I was very surprised when the Johnny Carson Show asked him to be on. I couldn't believe it. That was a blast. My family all thought it was hilarious. When he started getting so much press and attention for such a silly thing, we were all so surprised.

I was working at a little coffee shop at the time. I worked the early morning shift and I told all my customers to be sure to watch Johnny Carson that night, because my brother was going to be on. The next day, people came in and asked for my autograph!

Today, anytime I tell my friends that my brother was on Johnny Carson, they always want to know why. And when I tell them, they all just think it is so funny. Stephen's sandwich really is the story that just will not die. It keeps going on and on and just when we think its dead, somebody picks up on it again and he gets famous all over again!" – Lynette Jenne Drake

President Nixon was still alive when I appeared on The Tonight Show. I have no idea if he watched me on the show. I hope he did, and I hope he got a chuckle out it. But I never heard from him, (except for my draft notice!) Over the years, I never tried to get in touch with Nixon. I never wrote him a fan letter to ask for an autograph or anything. Who needs an autograph when you have the guy's half-eaten sandwich?!

A short time after the show, I went to a comedy club in Springfield to see a friend of mine, Barry Martin perform. He was one of the comedians, and we knew each other. He was in the same fraternity as I was, and I visited with him before the show. When he got up on stage, he introduced me to the audience and told them I had been on the Johnny Carson Show. Later, a female comedian came out and started good naturedly ribbing me, saying, "You S.O.B.! I've been trying to get on that show for 20 years and it just fell in your lap! You got on with your little sandwich!"

All the attention was great for my side business as a disc jockey. I billed myself as "SJ the DJ", which I had on my DJ van's license plate. During almost every event I did, whether it was a wedding reception or a graduation party, someone would get the mic and tell the audience, "This is the guy who was on the Johnny Carson show!" That was usually followed by someone coming up with the "original" idea of taking a bite out of a sandwich and giving it to me. I say "original" idea because I ended up being inundated with partially eaten sandwiches. Wherever I went, someone offered me a part of their sandwich, and I graciously took each one home…and fed it to my dog!

Over the first 25 years that I had kept the Nixon sandwich in my parents' freezer, every now and then, Mom would say, "Stephen, do you still want me to keep this sandwich?" She never asked me again after the Carson show. She knew it was something I was never giving up.

As the years went on, I continued to watch The Tonight Show. As I watched, I always thought to myself, "I had my elbow on Johnny's desk. I sat in that chair. I know what goes on backstage and what everything looks like." It was an experience I will never forget.

My conversation with Johnny lasted just eight minutes, but it was eight minutes that really had a huge impact on my life. I had held onto the Nixon sandwich for 28 years when Johnny Carson had me on his show. If Johnny thought 28 years was impressive, I wonder what he would think today, as the sandwich and I celebrate our 60th anniversary together!

Johnny Carson really had a lot to do with my Nixon sandwich being the story that never ends. When Johnny announced his retirement, it seemed that every newspaper and radio station wanted me to look back and relive my time on his show. The same thing happened in an even bigger way when Johnny died. The requests for interviews poured in, just like they did when President Nixon passed away. When Richard Nixon passed away on April 22, 1994, his sandwich had been in my freezer for more than 34 years.

CHAPTER SEVEN – HOLLYWOOD IS CALLING...AGAIN

In January 1989, I was totally shocked when entertainment booker Fred Puglia invited me to participate as a "celebrity" at the Decatur Celebration. For the past few decades, that event has drawn crowds of over 300, 000 people to Decatur.

Each year, the Celebration featured many big name, headline performers and musical acts. I knew I didn't fall into that category so I asked Fred why he was calling me. He explained that he looked at the Celebration as "a walking Ed Sullivan Show" and while the big name acts get most of the attention, the thing that made it special was many other "more unique acts". He said that my Nixon and Johnny Carson sandwiches were as unique as they come...and that he would even pay me!

While I was surprised when Fred called me in 1989, I thought it would be funny if I returned the favor...in 2020. When we called, Fred's first response was, "Steve who?"

Then he let out an enormous laugh when he realized he was talking to the "celebrity" he had booked 31 years earlier! Here are a few of his comments:

"I saw Steve on the Johnny Carson show and I knew right then that I had to get him for the Celebration. I liked unique acts. I like quirky. I once brought in a guy who collected rocks that looked like food! Another year, I had someone from Project Bluebook bring all of their flying saucer memorabilia. So I knew Steve would be perfect, and he was.

The Decatur Celebration had eleven stages of music, but I didn't look at the Celebration as a music festival. I saw it as a street festival that included music. There is a big difference. As people walked from one stage to another, I wanted them to see different acts right there in the middle of the street. I wanted to have a smorgasbord of entertainment. Those unique acts like Steve put a personality to the event.

Of course Steve didn't have an actual act. He was just himself and he talked about his sandwiches and his experience on the Carson show. And he mesmerized the people! People were in line to see him open his little cooler to show them his sandwiches!" – Fred Puglia

While Fred booked me in January, the actual event wasn't until August. In the week before the Celebration, as I watched the temperature soar to near 100 degrees, I worried about how I would keep my sandwiches frozen over the course of the three day event.

As soon as I got to the Celebration, I told one of the workers that I needed ice. They said it was only for the celebrities. I tried to explain that I was actually a participant in the Celebration, but they still said I couldn't have any ice. When Fred Puglia found out about my problem, he made sure I got all the ice I needed.

Fred got me set up with a booth that included a table and big sign that read "Celebrity Sandwich Man". I also put a smaller sign on my cooler. I made sure each sandwich was covered in ice, and if someone stopped by and wanted to see one, I carefully set it out. I took it out of the cooler for very short periods of time, but I never took the actual Nixon sandwich out of the jar.

I was surprised at how many people stopped by my booth. I was even more surprised at how thrilled they all seemed just to meet me. They truly made me feel like a real "celebrity"!

Comedian Henny Youngman was one of the "real" celebrities featured at the Celebration. Fred Puglia arranged for me to meet Henny, and made sure that I had a fresh sandwich with me when I did. Henny was known for his famous line, "Take my wife, please." I made him laugh when I said, "Henny, take a bite, please!" It was my third celebrity sandwich.

I added a fourth sandwich when professional golfer Sandra Palmer came to Springfield to play in an LGPA tournament. Sandra won the first Rail Golf Championship in Springfield in 1976, back when the tournament was named the "Jerry Lewis Muscular Dystrophy Classic". Sandra Wheeler, the director of the tournament was a close friend of mine. When she found out I was celebrating my birthday during the tournament, she asked Sandra Palmer to present me with a half-eaten sandwich. She actually gave it to me on the putting green, in front of a large crowd! It was a funny birthday gift…that I still have.

In March of 1990, my collection grew to five celebrity sandwiches, and the fifth one was "peculiar", to say the least. I had gone to the Ground Round restaurant for dinner, and as soon as I walked in, a group of guys called me over to their table. One of them was Curt Anderson and another was Stu Allen. Curt was program director and Stu was a DJ for WCVS radio in Springfield. They wanted to introduce me to their "special guest", who was dining with them.

That guest turned out to be "Tiny Tim". Known for his huge hit "Tip Toe Through The Tulips", Tiny was in town for a promotional appearance for the radio station. Stu Allen said, "We just had to get you two guys together."

Of course, The Tonight Show played a big role in Tiny Tim's life as well. He actually got married on the show! More than 45 million people tuned in to see Tiny Tim and

Miss Vicki's wedding on December 17, 1969. At the time, that was the highest-ever rating for a talk show.

I sat down next to Tiny and told him about my experience on The Tonight Show. He just laughed and laughed. He had already finished eating, but they ordered another tomato and lettuce sandwich for him so he could add it to my growing collection. When they handed it to him, it was like he had not eaten all week. He took three huge "chomp, chomp, chomp" bites, and had almost consumed the entire thing before he gave me the small portion that was left. And before you ask…yes, I still have it.

You can see a picture of Tiny and me in the photo section of this book. Well, it's kind of a photo of us. The person who took the photo only got half of me in the picture! You have to remember that all of this, all of my meetings with Nixon, Johnny Carson, Henny Youngman and Tiny Tim were long before our cell phone cameras. I also never dreamed I would have a book about my life. If I had known, I would have tried to get more photos. Back then, we didn't take photos of everything like we do today. We didn't have quality cameras on our phones. Heck, we didn't even have phones!

Also in 1990, a TV show called "America's Funniest People" called. Dave Coulier, who played Joey on "Full House", was a co-host. They did an interview with me over the phone, but apparently they weren't interested or impressed. At the end of our conversation they said, "We will probably pass at this time." I said, "Well, that's totally fine. You called me. It's no big deal to me," and I hung up.

Two years later, a trivia book called "What Counts" featured my Nixon sandwich. A lot of radio disk jockeys read that book and used the trivia on their radio shows. That led to many of them tracking me down to do phone interviews…again… for their shows.

In May of 1994, I was featured in the famous syndicated newspaper cartoon, "Ripley's Believe It or Not." I was, and still am, a "Ripley's Believe It Or Not" fan, and I collected all of the Ripley's books. So, it was quite an honor for me when they featured me in their newspaper comic. They drew a cartoon showing the sandwich in a refrigerator with a sign reading, "Don't Eat!"

In 2005, Troy Taylor included me in his book, "Weird Illinois". I guess I was honored to be in a book that spotlighted the weirdest people and places in the state of Illinois! But that book somehow ended up in the hands of a producer for the Game Show Network's "I've Got a Secret" show. I had grown up watching the original "I've Got a Secret", and this was an updated version of that classic program.

On March 3, 2006, I was again flown to Hollywood to appear on the game show. I carefully packed the Nixon sandwich in a Playmate Igloo cooler and took it with me as a carry on. I wasn't about to let it out of my sight as part of the "Checked-In" luggage!

During the show, celebrity panelists including Suzanne Westenhoefer and Jermaine Taylor attempted to guess what my "secret" was. The only clue the panelist had was that my "secret" was something of historical value. After asking me a series of "yes" and "no" questions, one of the panelists thought that since I was from Springfield, Illinois, maybe I had the bullet that killed President Abraham Lincoln!

After their time runs out on asking you questions, and if the panelists are unable to guess your "secret", then you win $1, 000 and a Hollywood dinner for two. Since I stumped the panel, I won. I was surprised when the dinner for two actually turned out to be $200 in cash. The Nixon sandwich was 46 years old when I was asked to be on "I've Got a Secret".

Other guests on the show with me included a woman who made bikinis out of dog hair and a woman whose "talent" was blowing up two balloons… with her nose! Yes, I fit right in with these folks. Each show also featured a celebrity. Ben Stein was on my show. His secret was that he had his pet dog stuffed. Ironically one of Ben Stein's first big jobs was writing speeches for President Richard Nixon.

In addition to winning $1, 200, the show also paid for my round trip flight to Hollywood. But they didn't have the budget that The Tonight Show had. They put me up for one night only, and then immediately flew me back to Illinois.

My short stay in Hollywood turned out to be a blessing. Just after I got home from the show, disaster struck…in the form of a tornado. The storm barely missed my house, but it knocked out the electricity. I frantically called my parents and was relieved to find that they still had power. So I rushed my Nixon and Johnny Carson sandwiches over to their freezer for safekeeping.

Before the power outage from the tornado, I managed to save the sandwich from another very close call. On Easter weekend, March 26, 1978, we had a severe ice storm in Central Illinois that took out our electricity for 3 or 4 days. But, thanks to my always prepared Dad, we were able to hook up a portable generator that kept the freezer running. We might not have had enough power to have lights in the house…but Nixon's sandwich was going to stay frozen!

When I wasn't around, my parents always did a great job "protecting" the sandwich. When I was away at college, or when I was in Vietnam, and even when I had my own home in Springfield, I knew that my sandwich was being taken care of, always safely in my parents' deep freeze. One time when my Mother was getting something out of the freezer, the jar containing the sandwich fell out onto the floor, but it didn't break. When they made those Musselman's Applesauce glass jars back in 1960, they made 'em to last!

In November of 2007, I appeared in the nationally syndicated "Hints from Heloise" column. At the time, I told Heloise, "The Nixon sandwich will be 47 years old this September. I have no plans to discard this historical piece of memorabilia, so it will probably outlive me."

CHAPTER EIGHT – THE SANDWICH THAT MIGHT OUTLIVE US ALL

I have never been married (so far). I hadn't planned to always stay single, but that's just the way it has worked out. But I found out that all my years as a bachelor allowed me to save and invest my earnings over my 31 years working at Hanson Engineers in Springfield.

In the summer of 2002, I decided to invest some of that money in a dream I had always had. I gave my resignation to my supervisor at Hanson. On my last day there, as I drove out of the parking lot, I looked back and saw my co-workers standing in the window, all waving goodbye to me.

I drove straight from there to my new interest and investment as a restaurant co-owner in Atlanta, Georgia. P.J. Van Beneden, a fraternity brother from college, and I became business partners as we opened a restaurant we named Burger Joe's.

We sold steak burgers, veggie burgers, chicken sandwiches, salads, French fries, and old fashioned milk shakes. The business was all delivery/take out. Our first business was just outside of Georgia Tech University, and we promoted delivery of our burgers until 3:00 a.m. We sold a lot of cheeseburgers and milk shakes to college students who were tired of only having pizza as a late night food delivery option.

Our initial goal was to sell Burger Joe's franchises. We were able to branch out with four franchises; three were in the Atlanta area and one in Virginia. But at the time, the price of beef and chicken had skyrocketed and the price of gas went even higher, making it very hard on our delivery cost.

Keeping reliable personnel was also a challenge. We'd hire someone we thought would be a good fit, and we'd train them for a couple weeks, but then they'd never show up again. It all got to be too much of a hassle for me.

I ended up selling 80% of my interest in the company, but did retain 20% in the naming rights and recipes. There are now two Burger Joe's left in Atlanta. I was in the restaurant business for eight years.

Believe it or not, we didn't have a buffalo barbecue sandwich on our Burger Joe's menu. Also hard to believe, that during the entire time I was in the restaurant business, I never gave a thought to that little half-eaten sandwich that was still sitting in my parents' freezer.

In November of 2007, I returned to the Sullivan High School to speak to an American History class. The school is located less than 100 yards from the spot where Richard Nixon gave his speech in 1960. After I talked to Carol Scott's class, we walked all of the students over to the park to see the little marker that's on the spot of the Nixon speech.

When I spoke to the students, I showed them the small paper plate that Nixon used for his meal. You can still see the barbecue stains on the plate six decades later. But I didn't bring the actual sandwich. I brought photos of it instead. My last two trips to California had started taking a toll on its condition. To help protect it, about ten years ago, I wrapped it in new cellophane and we put it in a sealed zip lock bag. Those didn't even exist in 1960! I have only opened the jar itself on very few occasions over the past 60 years, and there was never any foul odor. But I intend to keep the sandwich frozen from now on…unless some huge television appearance or something similar comes along again!

It was fun talking to the students. But I also found it a little challenging. Many of them had little knowledge of who Richard Nixon was, and I was even more surprised that they didn't know Johnny Carson at all! I guess fame really is fleeting.

During my retirement years, I served six years on the Alumni Board of Directors at my alma mater, the University of Central Missouri. In October of 2019, I was one of the first six TKE alums elected to the Delta Lambda chapter's Hall of Fame at Central Missouri. I've been a season ticket holder for basketball and football for the past 25 years. I've only missed one college homecoming since I graduated, and I had a pretty good reason for not being there. I was in Vietnam.

I've spent most of the past decade caring for my parents. I had to admit Dad to an assisted living facility, where he lived for three years before he passed away in January of 2016. He had a full military funeral and is inurned at Camp Butler National Cemetery in Springfield. Dad was 98.

In August of 2016, I admitted my Mother to the same facility where Dad had lived. As I write this, she continues living there and will turn 100 on Thanksgiving Day, 2020.

Six decades have now passed since Richard Nixon spoke in Sullivan. Many of the people who were there are now gone. And most of those who are still around can't remember what he talked about in his speech. But for the past 60 years, they have never forgotten that I was the one who "rescued" his sandwich!

Why did I keep the sandwich all these years? That's very simple. It was fun. I've always had fun with it. I never thought of myself as a celebrity. I never took any of it (or myself) very seriously. It got me a couple of free trips to California and helped me meet some pretty big stars. Of course Johnny Carson is a legend, and I was honored to be on his show. I looked at it all as an adventure. It was exciting, but it was just good, clean fun.

Andy Warhol once said, “We all get our 15 minutes of fame.” I guess I got a few more minutes than the average person…all because of a crazy sandwich.

Over the years, just when I thought I had given my last interview, my phone rings again. It seems to be “the sandwich story that just won’t die!” If any sort of milestone occurred, the media wanted to revisit my sandwich story, and me. It started eight years after I took the sandwich, when Nixon was finally elected President; then when he resigned from office, the calls came again. They continued with almost each Presidential election every four years. When Nixon passed away, I got many requests for interviews. With my Tonight Show appearance, I got associated with Johnny Carson, so when he retired, the calls came again. The same thing happened when Johnny passed away.

Today, the Nixon sandwich still sits quietly in my freezer…in the same applesauce jar we first put it in back in 1960.

THE LAST BITE

I was 23 years old when Steve Jenne appeared on "The Tonight Show, starring Johnny Carson."

Steve and I were from the same hometown of Sullivan, Illinois. He was quite a bit older than I, and since he had moved from Sullivan many years earlier, we had never met.

The night of his TV appearance with Johnny Carson, I had one of my first VCRs rolling. (I still have that original video tape.) As I watched the show, I couldn't believe that a man from our small hometown was on national TV, casually bantering with Johnny Carson! From that moment on, I was fascinated with Steve Jenne's story.

It would take another 20 years before I met Steve in person. By then, I was a TV news reporter/anchor, and I decided to try to find Steve. I ended up doing a couple stories with him, and each time he talked about his sandwich collection, the more captivated I became.

While his Nixon and Carson sandwiches got the most attention, the one in his collection that meant the most to me was Tiny Tim's. I had always been a huge fan of Tiny, and when Steve showed me his sandwich, I said, "Be sure to leave this one to me in your will!"

Steve and I stayed in touch, and six years ago I filmed a TV pilot for a show called "You Collect What?!" It was about people who collect unique items. Of course, Steve was the first person I called.

A few years ago, I retired from my television work and became an author. As the 60th Anniversary of Richard Nixon's visit to Sullivan approached, I wrote to Steve and told him I would like to turn his life story into a book. He was quite surprised, and did not jump at the opportunity. His exact words were, "You must be crazy." Imagine how I felt...the guy who has kept a half-eaten sandwich for 60 years...was calling ME crazy!

But after thinking it over for a few weeks, Steve finally agreed to my request.

While the "Nixon sandwich" might have changed Steve's life – it should not overshadow his entire life. After putting the sandwich in the freezer, Steve gave very little thought to it as he went on to live a very full and interesting life, that included serving his country in Vietnam, a very successful business career, and honoring and caring for his parents throughout their lives.

In my own life and career, I've been blessed to meet Presidents, sports legends, and music and movie stars. But I have never met anyone who was more interesting than Steve Jenne.

What a great guy you are Steve. Thank you for letting me help tell your amazing story. It has been an honor. Let's get together sometime soon. I'll buy lunch, as long as it's a big...pizza.

– Scot England